Art-Dialogue-Education

Disciplines, Fields and Change in Art Education

Volume 2
Aesthetics and Art Histories

Editors
Jacquie Swift &
John Swift

Series Editor
John Swift

Art-Dialogue-Education
Series Editor: John Swift

R27 136X

Disciplines, Fields and Change in Art Education
Volume 2 Aesthetics and Art Histories
Editors: Jacquie Swift & John Swift

Published by ARTicle Press.
First published in 2000

Cover by John Swift
Typeset by Alastair Scruton
Printed by Wolverley Studio Press Ltd

ISBN: 1.873352.18.2

Contents

Preface

The Art-Dialogue-Education series concentrates on material specifically centred on the practices and theories that inform fine art and art education. Generally, a series of conferences in either area acts as the initial focus, where invited papers are submitted for potential publication. In addition researchers are invited to submit chapters where their study is particularly relevant. The books promulgate the research activity of the Department of Art of the University of Central England, but also offer publishing opportunities to other artists and academics by contributing either papers to conferences or chapters to books. In this way it is intended to form a high quality national picture of some of the prevailing ideas, arguments and solutions in art and art education before and after the Millennium.

This book is the second volume of four entitled *Disciplines, Fields and Change in Art Education*. The themes of the eight conferences that feed the books explore the ways in which disciplines or fields of study have influenced art education and have been influenced in return. Thus the series began with concepts of how art education might be understood as a field of study and through some of its defining disciplines; specifically its relationship to art practice, and how it is affected by its split responsibility between art and education. This second volume examines the roles of aesthetics and art histories and their interplay with art education bringing to the fore a multi- or cross-disciplinary awareness. The third volume will examine perceptions of the disciplinary functions and changing importance of psychology, art therapy, and sociology and the ways they have developed into or across new areas in their effect on art education. The fourth and final volume of this series will be centred on specialist responses to the topics of each preceding volume and offer a plenary summation of current thinking on how disciplines or fields that are currently 'pure' or 'mixed' in their application have purchase within art education. The series will attempt to resolve whether change is needed or whether this is happening without pre-planning, and point to the richnesses that feed into and from the field of art education.

Whilst the whole series plans to offer a critical overview of the roles of disciplines and other fields of study on art education, arguably more fundamentally, the view of the usefulness of disciplines is called into question, and contrasted with the use of fields of study, or cross- or multi-disciplinary areas. The fragmentation of certainties in content or in method is considered. The ways in which thematic aspects that cross boundaries contrast with methods that function best within boundaries, and their respective strengths and weaknesses, will be explored. At the same time an open view on the usefulness of other disciplines or studies is maintained as a *leit motif* running through the whole series.

The first volume raised common issues within and across chapters, not least in the variety of ways that the terms 'discipline' and 'practice' were used, and we suspect that the multiplicity of positions that to some extent have defined the terminology of aesthetics and art history will also grow rather than diminish. What is less clear at present is whether this is beneficial, damaging or has no qualitative effect. In a world of fixedness and certainty the varied uses could be categorised as sloppy linguistic definition, but in a postmodern climate of relative, non-hierarchical and non-universal claims, definitions appear to reflect the contexts in which they function rather than any shared etymological root. As some disciplines lose their rigidity, boundaries and separateness and are permeated by other disciplines or fields of study, the use of neologisms flourishes and with it, the redefinition of terminology. This diversification is echoed in the changing roles that aesthetics, and what now more exactly is termed art histories, have taken upon themselves. This volume whilst showing to some extent the different positions of meta-theory, theory tied to practice and theory as practice, simultaneously presents a seeking for fluidity between disciplines and a movement towards an acceptance of hybridity and what this might imply. This raises the irony in using single disciplinary terms in the subtitling of the books - art education, art practice, aesthetics, art histories, psychology, art therapy and sociology - in that if the findings of the future volumes tally with the first two, the titles are mere 'umbrella' terms. In this they serve as a useful guide to what one might expect to find, but simultaneously mask the diversity the terms encompass.

We hope you find this volume interesting and challenging, and that it acts to extend the ways in which we commonly think of art and education.

John Swift.
Series Editor.

Aesthetics and Art Histories:
Introduction

Jacquie Swift

None of us can ever retrieve that innocence before all theory when art knew no need to justify itself, when one did not ask a work of art what it said because one knew what it did. From now to the end of consciousness, we are stuck with the task of defending art. We can only quarrel with one or another means of defence. Indeed we have an obligation to overthrow any means of defending and justifying art which becomes particularly obtuse or onerous or insensitive to contemporary needs and practices.

Susan Sontag 'Against Interpretation', *Evergreen Review*, 1964.

Aesthetics and the History of Art are disciplines totally reliant on the art product for their existence, but like all established traditions of inquiry have themselves tended to prescribe what is considered to be legitimate research within recognisable disciplinary frameworks. This has given rise to certain theoretical assumptions which underlie judgements made about art works (and artists) and it is necessary to repeatedly take stock of current positions. Disciplines as well as being methods of research are also ideological practices whose products constitute specific fields of meaning based on discourses. The more complex society and its art forms become, the more the relevance of these disciplines shifts, and it is this continual shifting, whether because of necessity or as the dictate of fashionable trends that forms the impetus for this series of books. This, the second of four publications continues an understanding of current art education as a complex field that is permanently engaged in coming into definition. One in which there is a constant scrutiny of changing themes of knowledge which might be capable of transcending current theoretical entrenchments and rivalries and therefore able to adopt emerging theoretical frameworks that enable strategic intervention in the ongoing debate. However, these need to be sufficiently flexible to offer the potential for dislocating dominant regimes of knowledge as well as the construction of different ones.

Both art history and aesthetics have long established frameworks of research and analysis composed of procedures and techniques which serve to manufacture a specific representation of art. But, it is vital to understand that there is no way that either discipline can be divorced from actual historical discourses. Writers and commentators of each historical period are constrained by the methods and discourses of that period and by its ideologies. There is, and has been, considerable variety as well as contradiction giving rise to irreconcilable theories of art and aesthetic value as well as differing social and political circumstances which have influenced the development of art history. The two disciplines, though irrevocably linked through the art object, have pursued different developmental routes.

Aesthetic theories are usually concerned with art, and high art at that, but can just as easily be about nature or mathematics. They have been an attempt to specify the nature of perception and the apprehension of a response to beauty; but the chief goal was to investigate the bases for shared taste and the perception of value. Within the Western tradition aesthetics is considered to date from the influence of Immanuel Kant's *The Critique of Judgement*, published in Germany in 1790, though the roots of modern ideas stem from earlier classical thinking. Considerable disagreement on questions such as the nature of art, creativity and the character of the experiences of beauty makes it impossible to generalise, but there has been a tendency to presume that a work of art's value transcends cultural and historical values. However, just what these values might be and who it is that decides them has been challenged at different times, and such questioning is particularly pertinent now, when the issue of cultural diversity is high on the agenda. Before Kant, Alexander Baumgarten published *Aesthetica*, a treatise not confined to the perception of art, but referring to the whole range of human perception and sensation; a discourse of the body which the Greek word *aisthesis*, from which it sprang, suggests. It is this very basic, even banal connection which has been continually overlooked by philosophers until recently.

Classical aesthetics sought to emphasise the organic harmony, integrity and totality of an artwork by creating an abstract, formalised theory. But, art objects are the product of experience, living and crafting. They are an engagement with the world and with materials, suggesting that there is a continual contradiction in attempting to regularise and contain an activity and a product which is unruly, unpredictable and as messy as the individual experiences which inform it. From the latter half of the 20th century, and following two world wars, a very noticeable transdisciplinary approach has been taken to attempt to reconcile these increasingly contentious and problematic ideas. Sociology, psychoanalytic theory, continental philosophy, linguistic analysis and the study of intertextuality have been some of the disciplines through which aesthetics has sought alternative interrogative structures, and feminism and post-colonialist theories have caused a revision of the hierarchies which prevailed within art and literature. The consequent cultural remapping that has taken place demonstrates that just as it is impossible to envisage a universal understanding of what makes great art, it is equally impossible to speak of art that might communicate to all people.

Art history borrows heavily from philosophy and the developments in the social sciences. It too involves cultural and political comment as well as visual and literary criticism. There has been a need for theoretically responsible art history to question the artist-centred account which has dominated the discipline since its emergence in Renaissance Italy when Giorgio Vasari set a standard of commentary which valorised the achievements of individual artists. Their place in a cyclical development with humanism as its chief element was central to the establishment of a canon of recognised 'great' works of art. This worked in tandem with the rise of connoisseurship, involving the making of judgements about quality for the purposes of attribution and relying on a recognition of 'quality' as well as 'value'. From a concentration on the uniqueness of the work of art in Renaissance Italy, to an expression of art as high culture formed in the German speaking countries, art history became understood as a manifestation of spiritual forces in 19th century Germany following the theories of the philosopher, Hegel. A review of the last century, during which it is considered that the centre of the discipline moved to the English speaking world - primarily caused by the political dispersal of scholars from Europe to Britain and North America - reveals a contradictory and turbulent period. It shows history complexly lived, and viewed, from a variety of cultures and perspectives, but also history which embodies vast political and social changes. In doing so it signals why it is potentially dangerous to assume sweeping generalisations, or indeed to accept totalising forms of knowledge.

Art, like history is made by people. There are specific individuals who operate under and within specific historical conditions and pressures with specific audiences. It is produced by real people in real material situations: and so is the writing about it. Art historians, like aestheticians, are also people positioned in a real world. What is ultimately significant in enabling an understanding of how and why certain discourses, texts and theories develop, is the role those material conditions have played and continue to play. The practice of living through them - and engagement with every day facts and values, mundane and rational constraints which make up the normal world of judgements, purposes and explanations, provides the practical framework required for making theories. It also provides the framework for modifying them. Feminism has had a profound effect in art historical discourse just as in philosophy, social, political and related epistemologies. Theories of difference have been part of the challenge to totalising forms of knowledge, and as hitherto unrepresented groups have gained political and social recognition, then a correspondingly increasing number of positions and perspectives have been and should be heard.

It is within this climate of cultural diversity that the essays in this volume are situated. Acutely aware of the need to re-appraise traditionally held values in the light of new critical readership, there is a noticeable call for re-reading, not merely old stances, but more recently forged theoretical concepts. In his exploration of the relationship of 'real time' as experienced in an art work and in the real world, Gérald Cipriani suggests that it is impossible to conceive the objective world and that of the lived world of duration as separate. Current 'technocratisation' of present day life seeks to control spontaneous or experienced flux and movement. In a carefully constructed essay, he suggests that earlier theories of metaphysics and phenomenology have been reduced to mere language in analytical philosophy and made meaningless, indeterminate and unstable in post structuralism. A native French speaker, he would seem to be singularly well placed to raise concerns which are currently exercising academics in all fields, but his insistence in identifying artistic experience as being close to motion itself because its existence depends on its relationships to extant prejudices, ideologies, everyday knowledge as well as to theories that are to be renewed or are not yet formulated, posits art practice and its products as pivotal to theoretical positioning. Judy Purdom's concern is also with art's direct relationship to real experience. Using a series of philosophical writings by Gilles Deleuze and referring to portraits painted by Francis Bacon, she contends that only art which disturbs, or disrupts audience expectations is truly creative. She pays attention particularly to the artist's deployment of paint to convey the sensation of being close to a face, or to the pain of another human being. The extremes to which its plasticity can be pushed and the subtleties of colour which can be organised are not merely conventions to be easily found in an artist's repertoire of techniques, but are the result of experimentation and taking risks with the materials in order to dis-cover resonances with that material and real life experience. Unlike the previous author she finds the instability and indeterminacy of continental philosophy to be a means of understanding this painter's work, which underlines the notion that different texts and theories develop for different ends and out of different material conditions. Bacon's empirical use of paint is of course not unique to him; to some degree the finding of 'equivalents' within the material is common to all artists. Although Bacon did not necessarily apply a typically Western convention of sequences, he still worked within painting conventions to realise new forms, and this enables Deleuze to move towards a recognition of painting's ontology. Its significance for art education are the importance of practice, theory and history, and that rather than students following ideas of easy iconography or stylistic fashion, they should be taught the tools and materials of their trade. In the taking apart of traditions and conventions and re-forming ways of making, real learning takes place.

The way that art itself develops; what John Roberts refers to as its 'going on' is the central tenet of the next chapter, 'After Adorno: Art, Autonomy and Critique'. In an admirable exposition of Adorno's *Aesthetic Theory*, in which he outlines the positions of the writer's detractors and defenders, Roberts claims that it is time to re-assess the theory in the light of recent art production and cultural comment. Theories of aesthetics have, in the past, been concerned with high art, but in the aftermath of post modernism new convergences in art have arisen. Not only have different forms of art emerged in contemporary practice, but so have new audiences. This set of different social conditions, brought about by a combination of new theoretical discourses including feminism, post colonialism, anti racism and queer theory has enabled art to challenge both the market and the academy and thus establish its own autonomy. In affirming that '[p]opular forms of attention are not so much the 'other' of authentic life, but the dominant space out of which aesthetic pleasures and values are formed and struggled over', Roberts repositions Adorno's aesthetics as one that is capable of embracing the conflict inherent within discriminatory processes. It is possible for the consumer to reap aesthetic enjoyment from forms which have been hitherto denigrated as low culture but within new theoretical frameworks are re-viewed and re-valued, just as the artist is able to take apart traditions and re-make them into new art forms. Adorno's theory accepts that the autonomy of the art object is produced out of the social relations which constitute art's institutions, therefore as the social conditions shift, so must the strategies of art and its theories. It is a carefully considered and courageous re-articulation of a position which has generated influence and direction during several decades.

These first three chapters adopt a stance which to differing degrees could be described as meta-theoretical, a re-theorising of an already established set of concepts. The next two chapters offer, in different forms, a rethinking of aesthetics and its relationship to art history, the art product, art practice and the artist. In doing so they provide a bridge from theoretical discourse as it stands in relation to other theories, towards an aesthetics and an art history which becomes more directly responsible to experience and practice.

Although feminist scholarship has been instrumental in the re-drawing of methodologies and perspectives in philosophy, it is only in the last decade, since 1990, that any real incursion has been made into the field of aesthetics. There have been and remain deeply entrenched assumptions about the universal experiencing of art and aesthetic sensibility requiring a paradigm shift which is only recently beginning to find some purchase. That women make, think and view differently from men is a concept which tends to be dismissed within mainstream aesthetics discourses. To perceive an art work not as an autonomous object, i.e., one answerable only to itself, but something that is an interaction with other experiences of the world is still contested.

Penny Florence feels that it is time to assess the potential of a 'differential' aesthetics. One that addresses and acknowledges that an individual's sex determines practice for an artist and a viewer. Acknowledging the difficulties that feminists have with established traditions of aesthetics; the association of femininity with the beautiful and an assumption of the universal reader - both demonstrably patriarchal in their construction - she suggests that established hierarchies have been an impediment to understanding the work of Barbara Hepworth. Not only have Hepworth's skills in combining scientific, artistic and humanistic epistemologies within her mature work not been written about, but the work has not been examined by feminists or analysed as a radical cultural achievement. She attributes the artist's marginalisation to the flawed logic of canonical inclusion, i.e., a work's value is determined by consensus and the fact that it endures in public opinion as valuable is proof that the original verdict was objective and valid. But as evidence demonstrates, the canon is not a simple constant but a perpetually changing theoretical construct which signals the way in which aesthetic theories can work to suppress art and artists which contradict them. Because Hepworth was classified as a modernist artist who pursued clarity and abstraction over tenderness or passion, she has been adversely criticised as not 'fitting' the accepted paradigm of feminine and as a result has not received the attention she deserves from mainstream or feminist scholars. Florence's insightful re-reading of the work presents an artist woefully neglected by theorists who have accepted prevailing opinion rather than examining her practice, lived experience and philosophy anew.

Theory can have the unfortunate tendency to denigrate the art work because it doesn't fit its frameworks. This has led not only to the sort of misunderstanding outlined above, but to alienation between theory and art practice. Many artists believe that theorists view their artworks out of context, analyse and explain them in language and for ends they themselves cannot recognise or even need in order to make art. By examining the writing of Arthur Danto, Helen Chapman goes a long way to explain how and why this can happen, even within the work of a philosopher considered to be so aware of art's needs. She identifies part of the problem as being the continuing prejudice in favour of the written word over the act of making. To challenge such prejudices in order to move the debate forward, she advocates a dialogue which is both responsive and responsible; one which engages with artists, art and history instead of holding on to aesthetic paradigms which presume a distanced and objective stance. The chapter concludes with an excerpt from a conversation between the philosopher Jean Luc Nancy and the work of a painter, which uses a variety of stylistic devices to attempt to enact the 'experience' of engaging with a work of art. What she finds most intriguing is the way attention is deliberately drawn to the inadequacy of Nancy's own discourse to find a language fitting to interact with the work. Once again, the writer and the artist are separated by the nature of the activities: one clean and removed, the other engaged with mucky practices and intractable materials.

The value of art lies in its resistance to conceptual abstraction and theoretical dogmatism and begs an aesthetics, a way of thinking and writing which is messy, irregular, unruly and contradictory. In other words, a way of forming a discourse which might be analogous not only to the art making processes, but to the experience which informs them. Awareness that different and diverse experiences and perspectives abound is an essential part of theory making. The final three chapters explore the formation of art historical and cultural theories as being themselves practices which interact with living and teaching to radically inform student awareness.

Gen Doy believes that theory enables students to form a greater understanding of culture, though theories themselves cannot be assumed to be merely self referential. Art works are never a series of discrete historical and artistic moments, but embody living processes and relate to the material world through which theories can be tested. Like Cipriani she is critical of post modernism's denial of the real or reality as being relevant as objects of theory, and takes a swipe at several seminal thinkers. For example, Edward Said has been unequivocal in his condemnation of intolerance and dominant political regimes, but is revealed as an autocratic and overpowering teacher who is unable to provide students with methodologies which they can apply to real situations. Instead, she favours a Marxist approach to teaching and understanding art history which seeks to 'situate the works in context in a dialectic way, paying attention to ambiguities, contradictions and tensions'. A piece by Roshini Kempadoo is used to show the way that the spectator can be a producer rather than a mere consumer and can do justice to a multiplicity of cultural meanings embodied 'consciously and unconsciously' within the work.

It is the way in which certain theories constrain the reading of art works that concerns Rosemary Betterton, who finds the meeting between the radical politics of feminism and the conservative discipline of traditional art history problematic. Citing Charlotte Brunsdon, she identifies a mixture of three student responses to her teaching of women's art genres: *deference*, when feminist readings of the text are accepted uncritically, *disruption* which can manifest itself as non-attendance, silence or confrontation and *disappointment*. The last, which she finds the most interesting, involves accusations that the art work does not appear to the student to embody the feminist meanings attributed to it, or that works that have intense personal resonance to the student might be dismissed by feminist critics. In taking the opinion of a well known scholar and setting it against that of a student, she seeks not to attack the scholar's view, but to assert that each response should be seen as 'proceeding from a different set of circumstances and knowledges'. This 'reading against the grain' not only allows for and legitimates multiple viewpoints, it interrogates relations of power - that of the teacher and student (implied in the title), the authoritative text and the interpretation, as well as that which exists between theory and practice. Academic writing is a learned form in which subject matter and method are intertwined. Making the choice is part of the method, and the form which conveys the meaning also determines the reader response. It is as true of writing practice as it is of making. The final chapter raises these issues as well as a number of others which have run through this volume. In doing so it directs our attention back to the first volume in the series, exploring the relationship between art theory and practice, and its place within art education.

In Marsha Meskimmon's opinion the structure of the university prevents genuine interdisciplinary activity and this has been exacerbated by recent pressures and codifying in order to allocate research funding. A polarisation of research and practice has ensued which she outlines succinctly, giving pointers to how this might be resolved through attitude and teaching structures, but with the caveat that art history and art practice are not the same. However, practice is not closed to dialogues with art history, neither does an artist refrain from integrating practice and research. Indeed, as she shows tellingly through the work of the American sculptor, Elizabeth King, it is in this way that an artist produces 'a dynamic space in which meanings are made across disciplinary boundaries'. Here, research is brought into contact with practice and with art history as part of the shared space of making meaning. Understanding the materials and methods of practitioners enables a fuller engagement with the product, awareness of the contexts and histories that art historians create. That art and its processes and products are visible and publicly recognised, is intrinsic to innovative making. As she eloquently shows, these links need to be 'explored developed and made more vital' so that reciprocal benefits can be realised.

The quotation at the beginning of this introduction called for art theory which is sensitive to contemporary needs and practices, and this collection of essays contributes splendidly to that aim. In the same short, but prescient article, Susan Sontag wondered whether it might be possible to develop a commentary on the arts that might *serve* the work of art and not *usurp* its place. Again, these essays would appear to find forms of commenting and ways of conveying meaning that strive to do just that. Instead of seeing art products and artists as getting in the way, confusing things, making them uncomfortable, these writers search for the means to express art's vitality rather than to deny or tame it. By not being afraid to engage with other disciplines, other practices and processes, they re-model ideas and words, taking apart traditions and conventions to re-fashion theories just as an artist will confront established art traditions, materials, methods and concepts to dis-cover new ways of making art.

Not only do these essays serve to raise critical awareness of how intellectual orthodoxies have shaped art's institutions and education, they challenge them to suggest the potential in new models and methods of theorising and teaching. Significantly, they acknowledge the primacy of the art product and process and the material conditions which inform and are informed by it, in a quest to disavow the polarisation of theory and practice. Furthermore, they seek ways of understanding how they combine in the making, reading and teaching of meaning in a changed cultural context which itself questions prevailing hierarchies of art forms and its diverse producers and publics. Art education is indeed fortunate in having this richness of theoretical debate to draw upon.

Art, Space and Time

Gérald Cipriani

Abstract

One of the characteristics of today's technocracies is a significant lack of interest
in our relationship to space and time. What used to be a main topic in traditional
philosophies (metaphysics) and the philosophies of experience (phenomenology)
has become a question of language in analytic philosophy and a meaningless
issue in deconstruction. Similarly, from what can be seen in art practice, theory
and education questions concerning the responsibility of spatiotemporality in our
understanding of art and ultimately of ourselves, are quasi-ignored. The naive
pragmatic instrumentalism of the most advanced capitalist societies and their
institutions, as well as the chaotic fragmentation that has infiltrated our everyday
and cultural lives prevent these questions from being raised. Both consumption
and aimless subjectivity are contributing to the disappearance of 'spatiotemporal
consciousness', and, at a more applied level, of our awareness of the formation
of meaning in art. This chapter aims to redress these views by arguing for a
suspension of time and space in the artist's or spectator's apprehension of art
which creates a particular and distinctive moment of linkage or emphasis.

The scope of this chapter is to redeem 'spatiotemporal consciousness' by
describing artistic experience in terms of 'suspension of objective time and space'
as conceived by the scientist. This experiential relationship to space and time is
what the metaphysician Henri Bergson calls 'duration', [1] and the
phenomenologist Maurice Merleau-Ponty the 'lived present'. [2] The aim is also to
show that any form of objectification relating to art 'differs from' or is 'disrupted by'
such a suspension, creating thus a spatiotemporality of another nature. Unless
one understands this phenomenon one will always run the risk of abusing and

misusing cognitive faculties, thus making the way for dogmatism, ideology or irrelevant intellectualism. The idea is to present artistic experience, that of the artist, or that of the spectator, or even that of an entire community, in terms of moment during which a particular relationship to space and time is bracketed, underlined, or simply accentuated.

To present artistic experience as the means by which spatiotemporal consciousness is developed, or even preserved, is like saying that the act of creation or perception of the work of art is suddenly going to make us become aware of an unsuspected aspect of our way of relating to space and time. 'Intuition' and 'pre-objective thought' correspond, respectively, to Bergson's 'duration' and Merleau-Ponty's 'lived present'. An attempt will be made, therefore, to answer the questions: What is the extent to which the experience of such a duration and lived present is stimulated by art? - *and* - How does it create a spatiotemporal consciousness?

In contrast to Bergson and Merleau-Ponty the point here is not to oppose the world of duration and lived present to the 'intellectual' world and the 'objective' one, respectively, simply because they ought to be understood in terms of complementary difference. Indeed, using the expression 'ought to' implies that the issue is ethical more than anything else. The possibility of conceiving the objective world as being separated from the lived world of duration surely cannot be denied. Indeed, this separation was operated by traditional metaphysics, albeit mistakenly. Rather, the issue is that we should not conceive them as separate because one cannot do without the other. To understand our experience of art in terms of meaningful movement that goes from one objective state, being, or significance, to another - in other words to understand it in terms of 'differing' - is to understand the relationship between duration and objective significance in terms of complementarity. It is like realising that one should never attempt to pretend to be the other, because their respective natures need each other in order to be different.

First, it will be necessary to clarify two key terms: 'significance' and 'meaning'. Significance, in the context of this chapter, corresponds to the idea of transcendent value ascribed to a phenomenon or a work of art. Once such a value is established

- it can be political, historical, formal or whatever - it goes beyond the experiential dimension of an individual's relation to art. From this follows that it disregards the situations of the artist, the work of art and the perceiver, as much as it ignores the communicant nature of their relationships during such an experience. A social significance for instance, is a value that one attempts to find in the work of art regardless of the historicality, 'culturality', or even 'sociality' of the interpreter, the work itself, and its creator. The same applies to the beautiful, the psychological, gender, ethnic specificity and so forth. The significance that the sociologist attempts to recognise in an art practice transcends the interpreter's actual viewing and that of the work being viewed. Such a significance exists, or ends up existing, outside an individual's lived relationship to art, but art's actuality is something that can only be experienced by human being(s). Consequently to look for a significance in art is to overlook artistic experience, whether perceptual or creative, as an 'affair of persons' - an expression that Eric Hirsch holds dear. [3]

Another way of defining 'significance' would be to say that it is 'objectified meaning', in other words a value that we extract from the work or that we project onto it, and which finally seems to be thrown against us or in front of us. Hence, the difference between significance and meaning: the former is disembodied from, or imposed on, the experiential dimension of the latter, creating thus different respective spatiotemporalities. To the notion of experienced meaning corresponds a proper lived spatialisation and temporalisation ('apertural space' and 'duration'), whereas physical space and time are, for the purpose of this chapter, measurable features constituted by significance itself.

Duration is here understood in terms of an infinitely complex movement that is created by series of different successive significances. This 'Bergsonian' movement is experienced by the mind/body in an immediate manner (intuition), while significances are stored (by memory) to constitute what we take as being the whole or reality itself. Consequently artistic experience understood in terms of such a meaningful movement, can only develop from the already known world of real significances that it disrupts, towards potential renewed significances. [4] It is the phenomenologist Henri Maldiney who uses the expression 'apertural space', which in this context is associated with this lived temporality and therefore distinguished from fixed physical space. [5] The former is space in the very process of opening from one aspect of reality to another future one, just as duration is the formation of time itself. [6] Another way of putting it would be to say that duration and apertural space are the *appearing* of spatiotemporality (meaning), whereas physical space and time are its *appearance* (significance).

The previous, though lengthy, exposition creates a position from which the phenomenon of the formation of meaning in art can be better described. The meaningful movement that is intuitively experienced by the mind/body petrifies in the form of past significance which is stored by memory. Such a significance becomes the trace of the actuality that used to be here and now, in other words, it becomes an absent actuality. This is when meaning distances itself from the point of departure. Objectified significances can take the shape of memorised colours and forms, historical knowledge, psychological explanation, sociological interpretation and so forth. These all belong to a world whose spatiotemporality can be measured, or fixed. Therefore, physical space and time ought to be understood in terms of 'environment' for further duration and aperturality to happen here and now, in other words for the formation of meaning to be possible. However, at the same time, meaningful experience can be interpreted as a potential significance, indeed, meaning is doomed to become objectified. It cannot escape the fate of losing its lived presence, which is precisely what constitutes its direction as a movement. In any case there is no question of a preferential dichotomy between duration/apertural space and physical spatiotemporality, anymore than there is between meaning and significance. Rather, it is important to talk about a necessarily complementary difference between the former and the latter.

To clarify further the nature of such an experience, it is necessary to recall Bergson's perceptual correlative of duration, that is to say 'intuition': it is an immediate contact with the world, or to put it differently, an immediate sensory-perception. The subject is so close to the object, that there is hardly any medium between one and the other. The subject almost becomes object and vice versa. Intuition is a matter of immediate awareness. [7] But when is there such an awareness? The answer to this must be, when there is 'coincidence' with the world. Phenomenologists talk about a 'connaturality' - a term borrowed from mediaeval Scholasticism - between subjective consciousness and the object of consciousness. [8] Another word for it would be an 'analogy' between the object of intuition and what is intuited. It follows that to understand artistic experience in terms of intuitive immediacy implies that during this very perceptual moment, art does not act as a medium for something to be re-cognised. Art has not yet become an object of knowledge. But this does not mean that in such circumstances art shows itself as an 'autonomous autonomy'. Rather, the viewer shares its autonomy because of what it brackets from the unnoticed world that is assumed to be known. During such an experience, the viewer is not dealing with a will forcing its way for the work of art to be perceived as an object of knowledge. On the contrary, there is a communion between perceiver and work of art, or the artist and making. Something is shared between one and the other. There is indeed an analogy between them. Such an analogy is therefore lived as a duration throughout the perceptual or creative experience. It might be possible to think that this moment of connaturality is motionless precisely because the subject comes close to 'fitting' the object, the spectator stands with the work, and the artist works within it. It certainly looks static from within the experience itself, because the experiencing spectator or the artist does not refer yet to external boundaries or herms such as social, formal, political, historical, psychoanalytical or whatever fixed significance.

Artistic experience cannot be conceived in terms of the precise phenomena of movement, transformation, becoming, unless these connections with external references are made. For example, it is only possible to realise that one is in a train in motion when one looks out of the window. Otherwise, the movement is merely 'felt'. There is only a sense of it, it is not realised, or rather, it is not objectified. What is known, is that one is in a train. Movement is being experienced, but the distance travelled is not known until an object, for example a tree can be seen going from the left to the right side of our window - in other words until reference is made to something external that can be recognised at one point, and which is moved to another point. Between these two points there is duration and something has changed: this is the formation of meaning. Poststructuralist thinkers would be eager to reject this image on the basis that it reduces movement to a linear spatiotemporality. In the context of this chapter the image of a movement that goes from one significance towards another potential one is used for the purpose of clarity. It does not simplify, it clarifies. The point is indeed to understand a principle in order to be aware of its unrepresentable potential complexity. Starting from the latter stage can only lead to unconsensual nihilism, where the imposing metaphysical subject is replaced by the impossible postmodern subject.

In the same way, an artist painting, a walk through an installation, the experiencing of a work of art visually, textually, or aurally, constitutes an awareness of an artistic experience. It is like being in the train, but without yet having figured out the distance of the journey between what was already known, with all those theories or past everyday-life experiences, and what is about to be known once the journey is over.

Artistic experience comes close to creating the thread that relates what will become the past objective world of significance (that is to say the image of the tree on the left side of the window in the train), to the future world of transformed significance to come (that is to say the image of the slightly older and therefore different tree on the right side of the window). In terms of space and time, artistic experience is close to motion itself, but motion whose vital existence depends on its relationships to both pre-conceived theories, ideologies, everyday-life knowledge, and renewed theories and cognitive attitudes to come. This suggests that there is bound to be a vital relationship between duration or the lived present, and the objective, representational, metaphysical world.

One could argue that there is nothing new about this, and that these ideas are found in different contexts from Aristotle's *The Physics* and Nietzsche's *The Birth of Tragedy*, to Heidegger's *Being and Time*, and Merleau-Ponty's *The Visible and the Invisible*. [9] However, and at a more applied level, it is precisely because of ignorance of these ideas that a misunderstanding about the complementary relationship between theory and practice has developed in the art world. Many theorists have used particular interested objectifying view-points in order to determine the nature of artistic experience, or more precisely, in order to predict the outcome at the end of the experience of duration. The list is a lengthy one, from Plekhanov's Marxism to Greenberg's formalism, from Freudian psychoanalysis to Saussure's structuralism. There are as many theories as there are categories and view-points from behind the window of the train - the form, the class struggle, the political, gender, the unconscious, language, or expression. This list also includes those who are radically 'committed' to the idea of duration or lived present. Bergson and Merleau-Ponty belong to it. [10] Moreover, it encompasses those who have recently systematised the notions of movement, flux and becoming, and who have brought them to the level of indeterminacy and instability, that is to say the poststructuralists and their followers, to mention only Gilles Deleuze.

It is an easy task to identify the dangers that are faced when dogmatically pre-conceived theories are used to determine the enduring movement from what is already known to what will be discovered with the work of art. The risk is that the phenomenon of the future differing from the past is concealed. The last image of the tree on the right side of the train window is concealed from the first one on the left. In other words there is no point from which to discern a change in the relationship with the tree, or conversely, with the work of art. The 'presencing' of contact with the work is in danger of becoming static. [11]

On the other hand, the question could be asked, what is wrong with being fully committed to the idea of duration and lived present, if it is what seems to be emphasised in artistic experience? The answer must be that such an enduring movement can only happen between one recognisable point and one yet to be known, in other words between what is already *known* about art (what it should be or what it shouldn't be) and what is to *be known* from such an *ec*-static experience. [12] Artistic experience described in these terms has therefore nothing to do with any idea of 'purity' or 'pure movement'.

Now as is well known, both Bergson and Merleau-Ponty tend to oppose discursive and abstract thought to 'intuition' and 'gestural language' respectively. [13] Bergson's concept of *intuition* is opposed to idealisation, conceptualisation, analysis, as much as *duration* is opposed to objectifying, quantifying, conceptions of time. If Bergson were followed, the result would be to oppose lived spatiotemporality in artistic experience to the kind of space and time that the theorist measures by using external interpretative boundaries, such as form, expression, gender, the unconscious, the social, etc. It would be like opposing lived spatiotemporality in art, to the kind of space and time that theorists fix when they measure the time and the distance that separate the beginning and the end of artistic experience, using particular view-points.

For Bergson, not only is intuition opposed to abstract thought, but it is the privileged means by which duration, viz. 'real time', can be understood. The Thomist theologian Jacques Maritain saw in this an unacceptable disregard for intellectual rationalism, which gave him the basis for his criticism of Bergsonism. [14] As a matter of fact, it simply does not make sense to reject 'intellectualism' and replace it by 'intuition', on the basis that any attempt to analyse experience comprehends a certain degree of 'intellectualism' or abstraction, and therefore cannot truly grasp experience itself. But is this Bergson's intention? It could be argued that he does not condemn analysis in itself, but only its inadequacy when it comes to working out change and movement. What is even more questionable in Maritain's argument is that he deduces that the only valid form of communicative thinking is abstraction or intellectualism. The fact that there is no such thing as pure artistic experience of duration, or pure connaturality between object and subject, the fact that there is always a degree of objectification in such an experience (otherwise it would be a meaningless experience), does not justify preferring the theoretical attitude as the only authentic thoughtful mode of communication. Any preferential dichotomy, whether it favours intellectual rationalism or experiential intuition can only lead to tension and alienation when it is a matter of understanding the relationship between artistic experience and its theorisation.

In fact one should keep in mind not only the complementarity between artistic meaningful experience and theorising objective significance, but also that the difference between the two is one of degree. One always carries an element of the other. There is more objective spatiotemporality established by analyses, than there is when one stands with the work of art and thus experiences an enduring movement. But it does not make any sense to favour one or the other on the basis that theory is not experience and experience is not theory, and that therefore one cannot accurately apprehend the other.

However Bergson in his 'Introduction à la métaphysique' argues that 'intuition', [15] which in this chapter is taken to be the passage of time from pre-conceived knowledge about art to future significance, cannot be transcribed by traditional ways of conceptualising, in other words by traditional metaphysics. [16] Only mutating and fluid concepts or metaphors are capable of evoking the experience of duration, but nonetheless always with a degree of distortion and imperfection. This proves that at some stage he thinks in terms of degree between conceptualisation and experience, and that the new metaphysics that he suggests is one which 'evokes' duration and movement.

One could understand this kind of metaphysics, which is less metaphysical than traditional metaphysics, as being the language of art, that is to say artistic experience itself. It is a language which brings subject, object, and also subject-matter very close to one another. It emphasises or intensifies and therefore brackets (to a certain degree) the phenomenon of duration. Artistic experience could therefore be called a 'language of duration' - not only a language, and not only a duration, but a 'language of duration'. [17]

This means that the space and the time involved in artistic experience are not like objects. It is a matter of continuous flux which opens a space or a distance from one, two or an infinity of fixed significances to other potential ones, other potential 'fixities'. It is a moving from one or several states to different states, and during such a movement becomes a waiting, experiencing, contemplating, creating.

But once again it is fundamental to see that the movement, duration, and flux that characterise art practice and perception, 'actualise themselves' precisely by means of these fixed significances that exist before an individual's experience of art, and potentially after it. There is a passage of time and thus a space in the process of opening, an apertural space, precisely because there is already a world of significances which situates the viewer, waiting to be surprised by an artistic experience which will itself lead them towards different beliefs, significant fixities, and therefore future environments. Each individual is always historically, culturally, socially situated before undergoing an artistic experience. They know how to recognise certain things in a certain way: to recognise a tree observed from the train just as much as to recognise, for example, form, history, expression or the unconscious in art. If this is not known, then it can be learned.

Between that initial moment when the looking at the work begins and that other when the looking stops, formal, historical, expressionistic, or psychoanalytic features have been deferred from one moment to another. This creates a different situation. But between these two situations there was the passage of time, and the opening of a space that separates the first image of the tree from the final image of it, or that separates what was already known before the work of art was seen, from what has been discovered from such an experience. Change, movement and duration become apparent, represented or spatiotemporally objectified precisely when one is in a position to relate different fixed significances to each other. However, 'during' this experience the degree of objectification is minimal, almost imperceptible. To develop representational thinking about artistic experience is in a way to measure the space and time that separate the past and future sides of such an experience. The mistake would be to forget that there cannot be any objectification, or representational significance without the unfolding of meaningful duration, and vice versa. Aristotle in *The Physics* declares that there 'is' time because of the soul. [18] Well, it could be said that the flux, movement or duration emphasised by artistic experience is in need of objectifications in order to develop.

Two neologisms can be made here. There are those who are committed to the idea of flux 'the fluxists' (and among them the poststructuralists); [19] and there are those who make a theory out of the fixity of the world 'the fixists' (and among them the philosophers of being, metaphysicists, modern theorists of art). [20] But how can it be denied that there is always a degree of flux and a degree of fixity in whatever attitude or approach is adopted towards the world or towards art? The answer must be that there is a difference in degree between artistic experience and objective thought about it. In addition, significant fixities allow meaningful flux to happen, and vice versa, the latter allows the former to be. In brief, it is possible to understand the relationship between the objective dimension of artistic experience and the experience itself in terms of degree, difference, and complementarity.

Artistic experience seems to be the privileged means by which such a flux, or duration is brought to our attention. This once again does not mean that art practice or artistic perceptual experience can do without what is fixed in space and time, in a transcendent way. Art can be thought of as a language of duration which 'pretends' to be objectifying. In the metaphor of the poet, the gesture of the dancer, the performance of the musician or the actor, the meaningful form of the visual artist, the space between the representing and the represented is reduced to its minimum: this is the phenomenon of 'presencing'.

Time is passing and space is in the process of opening: duration and apertural space. They have not been measured yet. The fixity of objective time and space is suspended. The moment during which the painter is painting or the moment during which the spectator is standing with the work, is a passage from what will become a past fixity, a past significance (e.g. the artist's and the spectator's social, cultural, existential or natural situation) to another (but this time potential) significance (that is to say the future objective interpretation or theorisation of the work). Duration understood in terms of moment of connaturality between object and subject, or in terms of flux and movement, not only compresses by its impact the still world of theories and representations, but also expands towards a renewed metaphysical world. The compression of the past and the expansion towards the future are like those images of a drop of milk falling into a bowl of milk. The phenomenon of meaning disrupts the still pool of knowledge and expectations, creating thus a variation of intensity which also expands like a splash. The tranquillity of the world of objective thoughts is ultimately recovered, but the world itself is transformed. A drop of milk has been added to the bowl. The work of art has just acquired a new significance. Time is passing and space is opening while the artist is painting, or while the spectator is looking at the work. This is what constitutes artistic experience as a language of duration: a gestural, metaphorical, meaningfully embodied language.

The spatiotemporal complementarity between the presencing of meaning and its past or future determined significances is a key element. Those who ignore it, such as ideologists and technocrats, believe that transcendent categories, pre-conceived theories, or measurements of all sorts can be applied systematically, as if the phenomenon of moving duration, or 'meta-fixity', or rather 'meta-substantiation', which constitutes part of our life and which is intensified by artistic experience, has no *raison d'être*. [21] Art is a significant means by which this metamorphosis is revealed: it begets an ecstatic movement precisely by suspending or disrupting pre-conceptions that are fixed in time and space.

To recall what was suggested at the beginning of the chapter there is no doubt that an overall 'scientifisation', or rather 'technocratisation' of life seeks to control for pragmatic reasons anything that has to do with flux, duration, movement. This pragmatic metaphysics seeks to fix values for consumption. The more there are, the better; therefore the less duration there is, the more efficient such an instrumentalism will be. But it would be equally wrong to think that a radicalisation of becoming, flux and movement, in the form of undecided theories of the undecidable is the best weapon against it. To understand artistic experience in terms of 'language of duration' is to develop a spatiotemporal consciousness, which is simply to understand the balance there ought to be between the representations people want to have and need to have, and their possible moments of transformation. Art still retains the potential to remind any one of us of this vital aspect of life.

References and notes

1   Bergson's concept of 'duration' (*durée*) is developed in his early doctoral work 'Essai sur les données immédiates de la conscience', in *Henri Bergson - oeuvres*. Paris: Presses Universitaires de France, Edition du Centenaire, 1991, pp. 51-156; but also in relationship to his vitalist conception of life in 'L'évolution créatrice', *Ibid.* pp. 495-500 & pp. 725-807; in 'Matière et mémoire', *ibid.* pp. 337-352; and in 'La pensée et le mouvant', *ibid.* pp. 1251-1432.

2   For Merleau-Ponty's conception of the 'lived present' see his *Phenomenology of Perception*. (Trans. C. Smith) London: Routledge, 1992, pp. 3-63, pp. 203-345 & pp. 410-433.

3   See Hirsch, E. D. in *Validity in Interpretation*. New Haven, Conn: Yale University Press, 1963, p. 23.

4   Bergson defines duration in terms of 'creative evolution' in which '... there is continuous creation of possibility and not only of reality' (own translation): '... *il y a création perpétuelle de possibilité et non pas seulement de réalité.*' Bergson, 1959, *op. cit.* p. 1262. In addition, '... the unfolding of duration in some ways seems like the unity of a progressing movement, and in other ways like a multiplicity of states spreading out' (own translation): '... *le déroulement de notre durée ressemble par certains côtés à l'unité d'un mouvement qui progresse, et par d'autres à une multiplicité d'états qui s'étalent, ...*' *ibid.* p. 1399.

5   Henri Maldiney evokes the apertural moment of the work of art, viz. the moment of opening, in *L'art, l' éclair de l'être*. Editions Comp'Act, 1993, p. 317.

6   Bergson's criticism of temporality defined by physicists is in fact a criticism against any conception of time relying on fixed spatialisation. The idea of 'apertural space' is not considered in Bergson's work and seems to be adequately suited to evoke the spatial dimension of lived temporality or duration.

7   See Bergson, 1959, *op. cit.* pp. 1345-1364 & pp. 1392-1432.

8   Mikel Dufrenne for instance mentions the necessary felt analogy between the poetical sign and the signified object. See Dufrenne in *Le poétique*. Paris: Presses Universitaires de France, 1963, p. 72.

9   See: Aristotle on the relationship between nature and change in *The Physics*. trans. Wicksteed, P. H. & Cornford, F. M., Cambridge: Harvard University Press, 1957, Vol. 1, Book 3; Friedrich Nietzsche on the co-existence between the Apollonian and the Dionysian in *The Birth of Tragedy and the Case of Wagner*. (Trans. W. Kaufman) London: Random House, 1966; Martin Heidegger's phenomenological description of the relationship between 'beings' and 'Being' in *Being and Time*. (Trans. Macquarrie, J. & Robinson, E.) Oxford: Blackwell, 1997, pp. 21-64; and Merleau-Ponty's idea of intertwining 'chiasm' between the objective and the perceived worlds in *The Visible and the Invisible*. (Trans. Lingis, A.Evanston III) Northwestern University Press, 1987, pp. 130-145.

10 See for example Bergson in 'La pensée et le mouvant', 1991, *op. cit.* pp. 1365-1392; for Merleau-Ponty's conception of 'lived presence' see note 2 above.

11 William McNeill, in his analysis of the idea of 'the glance of the eye' in the philosophy of Heidegger, talks about 'the event of presencing' which is associated with the latter's conception of '*Ereignis*'. See McNeill in *The Glance of the Eye*. New York: State University of New York Press, 1999, p. 116.

12 The prefix 'ec' refers here to its Greek etymology (ek) which means 'outside' or 'from'.

13 Bergson develops fully his conception of 'intuition' in 'La Pensée et le mouvant', *ibid*. pp. 1345-1364. Merleau-Ponty's idea of 'gestural language' is presented in 'The body as expression, and speech' from his *Phenomenology of Perception*. 1992, *op. cit* pp. 174-199.

14 See Jacques Maritain in *La philosophie Bergsonienne - études critiques*. Paris: Librairie Valois, 1930, pp. 147-206.

15 Although there are many points of disagreement between the two, Bergson's

work as a whole greatly influenced Deleuze's decentering philosophy of becoming, from *Le Bergsonisme*. Paris: Presses Universitaires de France, 1966 to *Cinéma 1, l'image mouvement*. Paris: Minuit, 1983, and *Cinéma 2, l'image temps*. Paris: Minuit, 1985. For a short account of the presence of Bergson's thought in the work of Deleuze see Constantin Boundas's 'The Bergson's series' in *Gilles Deleuze and the Theater of Philosophy*. Boundas, C. V. & Olkowski, D. (Eds.) London: Routledge, 1994, pp. 103-106. See also Marie-Claire Ropars-Wuillemier's, 'The cinema, reader of Gilles Deleuze' in *ibid*. pp. 255-261.

16   In a section called 'Introduction à la métaphysique' from 'La pensée et le mouvant', Bergson not only emphasises the fact that traditional Western metaphysics relies heavily on 'pre-existent concepts' and 'symbols' thus making it impossible to grasp movement accurately from within, but he also rejects Kant's critical philosophy for its 'subjective relativism'. See Bergson, 1991, *op. cit*. pp. 1392-1432.

17   Such an idea was already suggested in a different context with different words by George Hamilton Heard in his account of the relationship between Cézanne's painting and Bergson's concept of duration. See G. Hamilton Heard's 'Cézanne, Bergson and the image of time' in *College Art Journal*, 16.1, Fall 1956.

18   Aristotle, 1957, *op. cit*. Vol. 4, Books 10 to 14.

19   Philosophies involving ideas of change, flux, or indeterminacy can be traced from the works of Siddhartha Gautama (The Buddha) to Heraclitus of Ephesus, or from Arthur Schopenhauer to Jacques Derrida; from Indian Heterodox philosophers to the Pre-Socratics, or from modern 'voluntarist philosophers' to the poststructuralists.

20   Some Indian Orthodox philosophies such as Samkhya are metaphysical systems as speculative as the Hegelian grand narrative of consciousness. Fixed systems can also be clearly discerned from Parmenides's philosophy of being to mediaeval Scholasticism and modern theories which, for instance, aim at defining what the reality of art is meant to be like. In the latter case the list of different perspectives is endless: mimesis, expression, emotion, language, gender, the unconscious, form, and so forth.

21 The Greek prefix *meta* is here used in the sense of 'change', as in the cases of *meta-tithèmi* (to displace) or *meta-noew* (to change opinion). See Martin, F. in *Les mots grecs*. Paris: Hachette, 1990, p. 105.

The Work of Art:
Francis Bacon and Creativity as Experimentation

Judy Purdom

Abstract

Francis Bacon's portraits scream; they are shocking, even inhuman. How do they work? This is the task of aesthetics: to read the eloquence of the paint and to bring out the philosophy in art. Using the work of philosopher Gilles Deleuze (1925-95), I argue that, where art is truly creative, it gets on our nerves. It is not a matter of representation but of experimentation. The implication for art education is clear. Learning is to confront the problematic of colour and line, not to learn the rules of the game but to do art. For that there is no method, only what Deleuze calls a 'violent training'[1]: to experiment, to invent - to disrupt.

The meanings, all of them lie in the paint, and they are in the paint not latently but in the impact upon our senses, on our nerves. Nothing in these paintings is more eloquent that the paint itself. [2]

Francis Bacon's portraits are horrible; they are strange, disturbing, and shocking. There is copulation, defecation and vomiting. Faces are distorted beyond recognition, the flesh is raw and meaty, and bones protrude. These are portraits of Bacon's friends and lovers - Michael Leiris, George Dyer, David Sylvester, Henrietta Moraes - but are they affectionate images? No. They are brutal and animalistic, we might even say that they are inhuman. Like them or hate them, one thing is certain; as the art critic David Sylvester notes in his curator's introduction to the 1998 exhibition at The Hayward Gallery, and which I quote above, they impact upon your senses, on your nerves. They hit you in the guts; they scream. What is Bacon up to? The standard reference for Bacon is the interviews with art critic David Sylvester, a wide-ranging series of discussions recorded between 1962 and 1974. [3] In these interviews, Bacon makes it quite clear that, though his portraits are very specific, they are not (as is obvious from the merest glance) illustrations or pictorial likenesses. He makes the distinction between paint which conveys directly and paint which conveys through illustration; the paint that comes across directly hits the nervous system, while the illustration 'tells you the story in a long diatribe through the brain'.[4] Believing that through the direct approach the artist can open up sensation and 'return the onlooker to life more violently' [5] Bacon attempts to do something quite 'irrational' from the point of view of illustration; he works against the conventional form of the portrait with the aim, not just of remaking the look of the image but of capturing the feeling or sensation of the subject. [6]

The two approaches to the face identified by Bacon - the illustrational and the non-illustrational, or 'irrational' - are echoed in the two poles of the face discussed by Gilles Deleuze in *Cinema 1*, the reflecting surface of the envisaged face, and the intensive face or close-up:

Sometimes painting grasps the face as an outline, by an encircling line which traces the nose, the mouth, the edge of the eyelids, and even the beard and the cap: it is a surface of faceification [visagéification]. Sometimes, however, it works through dispersed features taken globally; fragmentary and broken lines which indicate here the quivering of the lips, there the brilliance of a look, and which involve a content which to a greater or lesser extent rebels against the outline: these are the traits of faceicity [visagéité]. [7]

This polarity is further elaborated in *A Thousand Plateaus*, in a chapter entitled 'Year Zero: Faciality.' [8] Here Deleuze and his co-author Félix Guattari distinguish between the socially produced face and the non-signifying head. The socially produced face is instantly recognisable: ears, eyes, nose, mouth; happy or sad, old or young, man or woman; student, worker, judge. There is a 'whole' face with an outline and features, a face that conforms to the perceptual and representational requirements of a determined identity. It is a finely crafted, disciplined organisation, produced within a rationalised social and theoretical milieu; the discourse of white, male and European, and as Deleuze and Guattari detail, of Christ as Year Zero. The conventions of this signifying faciality demands that portraiture deal in the familiar, and rather comfortable, form of recognisable likeness, and that that likeness carries intimations of character. One only has to look at portraits of kings, intellectuals and statesmen, or indeed film stills or advertisements to see what is meant by the face as a socially produced organisation or, as Deleuze and Guattari point out, that 'The face is a politics.' [9] The head is quite different from the readable face of the regal portrait or the obvious signification of the advertisement. For Deleuze and Guattari the head is a 'horror story.' [10] It is fleshy and animal, a featureless and ill-defined close-up: it is a meaty surface with 'pores, planes, matts, bright colours, whiteness, and holes...' and 'a lunar landscape' where there is no distinct outline or features, just texture and expression. [11] The face has perspective, it is generalised and human, meaningful as a realistic and faceified [visagéifée] or visualised representation. The head loses all perspective and is a close-up; a direct rendering that confronts the materiality of the face. Features are indistinct and age and gender unidentifiable, but there is a particularity in the colour and texture that is disturbing, shocking and often horrible.

Clearly Bacon is not interested in making the clichéd portrait that reflects and illustrates social status and political values but in the non-illustrational pole of the face; the fleshy head. While the illustrational might be understood as a top-down approach because here the artist is manipulating paint to make a form that reflects a certain perspective - social, political or formal - and that accords to already rationalised principles, Bacon adopts a bottom-up or non-illustrational approach and returns to an image that works at the level of its material and that refers only to its own composition. Bacon himself defines the difference between the illustrational and the non-illustrational as the difference between painting that works through the intelligence and that which works directly:

Well, I think that the difference is that an illustrational form tells you through the intelligence immediately what the form is about, whereas a non-illustrational form works first upon sensation and then slowly leaks back into the fact. [12]

What becomes important in the non-illustrational approach is not shape but colour and texture; not look but sensation. The fleshy morass of the Bacon face is very like the face as close-up. In contrast to the social portrait, it is not an organised structure but an intensive mass of colour and line. It is an ill-defined, fleshy surface with no definite features - a moonscape of pores and planes, flaky matts and horrible shiny bits, splodges of pink and blue and grey... a lunar landscape; or meat. Sometimes the pink glows flushed with pleasure (fresh meat); sometimes it is dull and grey with tiredness, or contorted by stress (rank meat). It is hardly a face at all, but a monstrous inhuman head, a composition in colour.

In his portraits Bacon is not concerned with drawing accurate representations of his friends, but with conveying sensation: their neurosis, anxiety or (rarely) their *joie de vivre* - their life. His are not so much portraits *of the face*, but *in your face*. Rather than the portrait being of the face, the face is itself the expression - an explosion of colour that quivers, convulses or cries. So, whilst, when we compare Bacon's portraits to the photographs which he often worked from, we can see a definite likeness and even a story - here is George Dyer on the toilet, there is Henrietta Moreas impaled to the bed with a syringe - it is the sensation that impacts: the orgasm, the vacant scream, the smile. On the one hand then, Bacon's portraits are absolutely specific to their subject and instantly recognisable - they are of Henrietta Moraes, George Dyer, David Sylvester...; on the other hand they are an abstract configuration of colour. Bacon himself describes his work as a 'tightrope walk between what is called figurative painting and abstraction' [13] and it is the tension between representation and sensation that marks out his work as a revolution in portraiture. But how does he achieve this? I want to argue that he distorts and even dissolves the conventions and clichés of more traditional portraiture in order to return to painting as an art of sensation. He returns to colour, line and texture and experiments with what paint can do, and it is from that abstract work that the figure emerges.

Bacon's methodology bears this out. He admits that he does not know in advance how the form can be made and that indeed he actively resists the notion of the pre-formed image. [14] He relies instead on the accident of the throw of paint and the contours that emerge in the differential of colour and texture on the canvas. He starts by throwing paint on the canvas and then manipulates this riot of colour: ragging and sponging, streaking, smudging and printing. And starting all over again. It is therefore the manual marks that open up the possibility of moving away from the clichéd figure because the features of the face are suggested by the chance chaos of colour and resemblance found in the eloquence of the paint and in particular in the sensation that colour produces. The cheekbone emerges at the conjunction of red and blue, and the mouth is hinted at in the smudged cacophony of pink and green, or a sweep that extends right across the face. Bacon rejects the rules of form that govern representation. Instead, he works with the materials, using the experimental patterns and rhythms of thrown colour to draw the face out of that chance formation and to create a pictorial image that is absolutely specific to painting. For instance in the interview of 1962 he describes painting a head where the features were forms that had nothing to do with eyes, nose or mouth but where 'the paint moving from one contour into another made a likeness of this person I was trying to paint.' [15] It is in this sense I want to argue, that Bacon is truly creative. The faces were never seen or imagined or thought before they emerged on the canvas and have no existence except their material existence as a performance in paint. Bacon thus creates images that he himself understands as 'completely irrational from the point of view of being an illustration.' [16]

In his emphasis on the power of colour Bacon echoes Cézanne whom, with the notion of 'colouring sensation' [*sensation colorante*] understood the task of painting as bringing life to the image. [17] Dismissing drawing as formulaic design and a 'bastard logic' akin to arithmetic and geometry, Cézanne discovered that the way to a full rendering of the sun, a tree, a rock, a dog... is colour: 'Colour, if I may say so is biological. Colour is alive, colour alone makes things come alive': painting, says Cézanne, must have an allegiance to a certain 'logic of colour.' [18] Here he is talking, not about colour as a signifier within a value laden economy in the way that red might represent blood, black infer night or white and light denote purity and truth, but about how the conjunction of planes of colour sets up rhythms and patterns which carries a certain sensation: the quivering of the lips, the brilliance of a look or the vacuity of the scream - the animated 'life' of the face. I see the same 'colouring sensation' in Bacon's portraits as in the last works of Cézanne ('Portrait of Joachim Gasquet' 1896 or 'Montagne Sainte-Victoire' 1904-6) because in both colour is used, not to emphasis the form but to produce sensation.

This homage to Cézanne is also a feature of Deleuze's own work on Bacon,

Francis Bacon: Logique de la sensation, published in 1981. [19] Here Deleuze is concerned to develop an ontology of painting and to explore just how a 'logic of colour' might work. He regards Bacon as a radical artist who approaches his subject, not as a factual object, but as an individual whose form depends on its immediate history and maturation. In other words, he argues that Bacon refuses the preconceptions about form that govern the objectification of the 'face as politics' and returns to the face in close-up - the face itself. Deleuze argues that by disrupting and dissolving the conventional form of the face with the chance throw of paint and irrational, manual marks, Bacon moves from face to head and creates sensation, not as represented or illustrated but as experienced. Two short quotes demonstrate Deleuze's position: 'It is thus a very special project that Bacon pursues as portraitist: to undo the face, to rediscover or cause to surge forth the head beneath the face;' [20] and 'Sensation is what is being painted. What is painted on the canvas is the body, not insofar as it is represented as an object, but insofar as it is experienced as sustaining this sensation.' [21] Without recourse to the determining framework of the representational model, Bacon is left to find the likeness that belongs only to colour; experimenting and inventing, seeing what paint can do, and using the force of colour to suggest the final image. It is this emphasis on the matter and work of paint, and in particular on colour, that fascinates Deleuze. He approaches the Bacon portrait, not with the question of representation 'Is it a good likeness?' but by asking the more interesting questions, 'What does it do?' and 'Does it work?' And, if it works - if it produces sensation - then 'How does it work?' He therefore examines Bacon's method and style in order to identify just how Bacon makes these strange portraits so powerful - and so horrible. He looks at what the paint is doing, and identifies its own logic - the logic of sensation. He is interested, not in painting as illustration, but in the work of the paint itself and its power of affect, and therefore in the peculiar ontology of painting. Deleuze looks at Bacon's techniques and style, and asks how Bacon's particular combination of colours and techniques is held together as the consistent composition which produces certain sensations or effects. For instance: he talks about Bacon's use of the armature which isolates the figure and detaches it from a space/time frame; he talks about how the figure is juxtaposed against the indefinition of the plain, bright coloured ground; about how the face is dissolved in a streaked and hazy curtain; about the tension between the figures in the triptych; - and about how the face is swallowed up in the chasm of the scream. [22]

It is the scream that so preoccupies Bacon and which is a recurring image throughout his work of the 1950s, notably in the series of Popes inspired by Velasquez's 'Pope Innocent X' 1650. The scream is precisely that sensation that is beyond any rational comprehension. How do you paint the terror of the scream? It is not the story behind the scream that is important - be it massacre or accident - but the catatonic spasm of the face and the open chasm of the mouth that creates the scream. The face screams when the mouth takes over the face and when we see the normally hidden glitter and colour of the inside the mouth. In other words, Bacon's task is not to paint the scream as an expression of horror but to paint the forces that make the scream - the strain of the lips, the hollow of the mouth, and the convulsion of the body. The scream is then a certain composition of the face, and a 'matter' of expression, and not an illustration or indication of the severity of an upsetting incident. In the interviews with Sylvester he relates how he was inspired by the still of the nanny screaming from Eisenstein's film, 'The Battleship Potemkin' 1925; by Poussin's, 'The Massacre of the Innocents' 1630-31, which he considered to be the best human cry in painting; and by a medical book on diseases of the mouth. But these were not carried into a scene of an equivalent massacre, but into a series of portraits of Popes, the most striking of which is perhaps 'Head VI' 1949, where we see the Pope isolated within a box or armature and where, like some perverse Cheshire cat, the face is dissolved in a shadowy curtain, to leave nothing but the scream. Even the Pope's robes echo on the contours of the mouth as if they too are propelling the scream out of the black hole of the mouth. The paint works to produce the scream as pure force, not to depict or illustrate but to make a sensation - piercing, shrieking and shrill - that refers only to the paint itself. With Bacon's scream in mind, we can then understand what Deleuze means when he enigmatically declares that sensation is not realised in the material but that 'all the material becomes expressive', and when he talks about the smile of oil, the gesture of fired clay and the thrust of metal - or the scream of paint. [23] The scream is not a representation or indication of horror as seen, experienced or understood but a much more powerful force. We cannot possibly understand the scream, and seeing the scream makes no sense at all. We can tell a story about the why and the where of the scream, but like pain, its force is its immediacy. We could say that Bacon celebrates or commemorates the scream. The force of the scream - the sensation - passes into the material and is conveyed in the coloured rhythms and patterns of the paint. The paint screams.

If painting is not to resort to representational systems it must stand on its own as a material art. It must not depend on the perspective of the viewer or the artist; or on opinion, point of view or personal experience; it must go beyond the human constructs of representation and stand as a monument to sensation. Instead of a concern with what can be represented in the sensible, it must deal with what can only be sensed. Deleuze's philosophy of art is therefore not an empiricism that uses 'lived' experience as its reference point, or a phenomenology that has recourse to consciousness - even if, as in Merleau-Ponty that consciousness is the ubiquitous 'fascination' of the artist. Deleuze thus moves to what he calls a 'superior' or 'transcendental' empiricism where, as he puts it, 'the work of art leaves the domain of representation in order to become "experience", transcendental empiricism or science of the sensible.' [24] The task of the artist here is not to paint a perception of the thing, or a sensation or feeling about the thing in the way that the scream as an expression of horror might be; that would be a resort to painting as illustration and therefore to re-present a perception or affection. Instead, the task of the artist is to make the material work and art stand on its own, just as Bacon does when he makes the paint convulse and scream. In *What is Philosophy?* Deleuze explains this as the artist wresting the percept from the perception, and the affect from affection, and making the material produce the sensation. [25] Bacon painting the scream is a case in point. As described above, Bacon paints the scream as pure force without any object, as pure horror; the scream not as it can be represented in paint but as it can only be sensed, and as it touches the nerve and hits you in the guts. The percept is not a perception. It is independent of those who experience it. The affect is not a feeling or affection, but exceeds any lived sensation. The work of art does not exist 'as seen', 'as thought' or 'as felt' - 'as lived'; it exists in itself.

How then is it that Bacon's portraits resemble their subjects and are easily recognisable? How can Deleuze say that the painting exists in itself and stands up on its own? First, Deleuze argues that habits of perception and representation are not so easily rejected. The task of the artist is a violent one, it is to wrest the percept from perception, to extract it and to capture it. Secondly he points out that to do that, the artist must start with the 'standard' representation and distort it, undoing the representation - the face - and allowing sensation - the head - to take over. In that gross distortion, easy to see in Bacon, all the clichés and conventions of the representational language of art are corrupted and the logic of representation made to stammer and tremble. [26] To a certain extent this trembling is a matter of style: every painter makes the subject their own, Bacon's Popes and 'Study for Portrait of Van Gogh II' 1957, being obvious examples; and every musician, even playing a standard or repertoire piece, makes their own rendition. The musical analogy is useful here because, if we think of the canvas like a composition of notes, and of each brush-stroke as a note, then we can see how the painter makes the canvas sing by making patterns of notes and builds up rhythms through consonance, dissonance, and harmonics. The painter makes connections, disconnections and conjunctions: there are rhythms and patterns, speed and slowness; spasm, flow, jolts, contortions; all manner of novel intersections of colour - all manner of new sensations, even within a given brief. This is why Deleuze can say that the artist is truly creative when she or he adds new varieties to the world; [27] when the artist invents new percepts and affects, and new sensations, when new ways of seeing and feeling are invented, and when the representational model is challenged and made to tremble.

In *Francis Bacon: Logique de la sensation*, Deleuze examines what he calls Bacon's 'operative' experimentation [28] and shows how Bacon disfigures the face in order to break with representation and to make visible sensation itself. Now if painting is to be operative it must have its own mans of expression and its own logic; and because painting is a material art those means are physical operations, and its logic the techniques of composition. For Deleuze therefore, art is crucially about materials and techniques, method and style, and about making material become expressive. However, this does not mean that painting should adopt a system or theory of form, but rather that it should be a pragmatics where form is the immediate result of 'doing' and practical experimentation. Deleuze evokes the image of the 'box of tools' to describe the work of the concept in a philosophy which demands truly creative thinking, and this same notion has resonance in the idea of a performance or action-led art practice where a basic knowledge of materials and techniques, and of form, is used in novel and interesting ways. [29] Practice is here not restricted by a given theory or by preconceived concepts but inspired by the flexibility and malleability of the materials and the skill of the artist. This notion of an operative theory-practice is characteristic of Bacon's work. Talking about Bacon's methods - the throw of paint - Sylvester asks if perhaps anyone could 'do a Bacon'? Whilst not ruling out the possibility that someone could come in and do it as well or better 'by chance', Bacon is adamant that his method relies on expertise; he must *know his materials*. [30] Although he wants the paint to have a look of inevitability and immediacy that does not mean sloppiness, indeed he likes highly disciplined painting - Velasquez, Rembrandt, Degas - and loathes what he sees as 'chancy' abstract expressionism. [31] He works by 'inspired chance' and the 'accident'. The throw demands control: choice of colour and consistency, decisions about the force and angle of the throw, and when to stop. Then there is the manipulation of the paint: the ragging and sponging; rubbing out, brushing; building up layers, thinning out areas. It is at once highly controlled and magnificently experimental. It depends very much on practice and knowing the materials, even to the point of knowing and accepting the fluidity and malleability of oils - Bacon calls oil a 'curious medium' because you never really know what it will do. The skill lies in knowing how to make best use of that suppleness; going with it, using the unknown and unthought to advantage. Sylvester suggests, to Bacon's enthusiastic approval, that painting is rather like playing a ball game. [32] Once you have mastered certain techniques, know your equipment and 'have got your action into a certain groove' - and don't think about it too much - you can start to be creative, even to do things that amaze yourself. You can start to experiment. You can take the materials to new unimagined extremes and do things that you would never have thought of. This is why Bacon thought that some of his best work - the stunning triptych (May-June 1973) of George Dyer's death springs to mind - was done when he was in his cups; depressed, despairing or drunk, simply not thinking too hard. Going with the flow. This of course points to the necessity of a rigorous art training in technique, in materials and in art history. It means giving artists a box of tools so that they can move from what Cézanne called the 'bastard logic' of the illustration to a 'logic of colour' and creativity.

Deleuze's move to an ontology of painting forces us to take the study of material seriously because the idea that the image emerges from material relations inevitably puts the emphasis on composition and techniques in painting. Bacon's stunning portraits are a case in point. However, experimentation demands investigation as well as speculation and risk and Bacon's box of tools encompasses not only his knowledge of materials but his conversance with the traditions and conventions of art, and his close observation and wide interest in visual practices - including photography and cinema. For instance, he admired the colour in Velasquez and Cézanne, the paint marks in Rembrandt, and the protrusion of the spine in Degas' 'After the Bath' of 1903; and as the interviews demonstrate, was able to articulate just why certain compositions have such force. He was also a great observer, looking at animal skins to think about the colours and textures of the human skin, studying X-ray photographs and butchers' meat for the relationship of bone and flesh, and analysing Muybridge's photographs of wrestlers for poses of the coupling of figures. Art education could learn much from Bacon's eclectic investigations with a view to promoting a broad visual education alongside classes in the use of tools and materials. The aim would be to teach the student to take apart visual traditions and conventions, and to examine them from the point of view of sensation rather than illustration - asking what they do, and how they work. Only then might they attain the same control that Bacon brings to his experimentation. Only then can the artist move the tradition on, not by emulating a certain style of fashion in painting but, in the conjunction of theory and practice, re-forming ways of making, pushing forward certain techniques and using the materials and tools of their trade to produce new images and to create new sensations. Technique and materials, history of art, and a visual education comprise three facets of the challenge to art education - to give the artist the tools with which to 'do' and to create, and to train the artist in techniques and skills which they can use creatively as a 'box of tools' that is at once both theory and practice. Creativity requires experimentation; only then will the true eloquence of paint be discovered.

References

1 Gilles Deleuze, *Difference and Repetition*. Athlone Press, 1994, p. 165.

2 David Sylvester, *Francis Bacon: The Human Body*. Hayward Gallery, 1998.

3 David Sylvester, *Interviews with Francis Bacon*. Thames and Hudson, 1975. This volume includes many reproductions of Bacon's paintings - many of the Pope series including 'Head VI' 1949 - as well as images that Bacon himself refers to, including Velasquez' 'Pope Innocent X' 1650, the still of the nanny from Eisenstein's The Battleship Potemkin 1925 and a detail from Poussin's 'The Massacre of the Innocents' 1630-1.

4 *Ibid*. p. 18.

5 *Ibid*. p. 17.

6 *Ibid*. p. 26.

7 Gilles Deleuze, *Cinema 1: The Movement-Image*. Athlone Press, 1986, p. 88.

8 Gilles Deleuze and Felix Guattari, *A Thousand Plateaus*. Athlone Press, 1988 pp. 167-191. In the chapter, 'Year Zero: Faciality', Deleuze and Guattari discuss the face as a 'whitewall/black hole' system, an 'abstract machine' which produces faces as a dimensionless and formless 'holey surface'; as inanimate, inhuman and a 'horror story'. They understand the face as, by nature, a close-up, by which they mean that it has no intrinsic organisation. The recognisable face with its distinct features is achieved by a socio-political overcoding which subjugates the face to the rationale of 'human' signification.

9 *Ibid*. p. 181. The formulaic representation of the socially produced portrait is the subject of Richard Dyer's recent book *White*. Routledge, 1997. Though Dyer is principally concerned with the cinematic 'Hollywood' image, in his discussion of conventions of the facial image he makes many references to fine art. He makes the point that white and light are significantly synonymous and that the portrayal of the face is underlined by this distinctive use of light in painting. White and light are used to infer the positive values of the Enlightenment - knowledge, truth and beauty; inspiration, spirituality and

sensuality. The racist implications are clear.

10   Deleuze, G. and Guattari, F. 1988, *op cit*. p. 168.

11   *Ibid*. p. 190.

12   Sylvester, D. *op cit*. p. 56.

13   *Ibid*. p. 12.

14   *Ibid*.

15   *Ibid*.

16   *Ibid*. p. 11.

17   Gasquet, J. *Joachim Gasquet's Cézanne: A memoir with Conversations*.
     Thames and Hudson, 1991, p. 154. Deleuze foregrounds Cézanne and
     'colouring sensation' (*sensation colorante*) in the preface to his own study of
     a logic of sensation, *Francis Bacon: Logique de la sensation*, where he says
     that aspects of Bacon's work 'converge in colour, in the 'colouring sensation'
     which is the summit of this logic'. See: Deleuze, G. *Francis Bacon: Logique
     de la sensation. Éditions de la Différence*, 1981, p. 7.

18   Gasquet, J. *op cit*. pp. 161-2.

19   Deleuze, G. 1981, *op cit*. Deleuze's treatise on Bacon is presented in two
     volumes, part one is the text, part two the paintings. This second volume is a
     useful visual index of Bacon's major pieces. The text is not yet available in
     English, however a rubric by rubric account which includes translations of
     many passages can be found in: 'Francis Bacon: The Logic of Sensation' by
     Dana Polan in Boundas, C. V. and Olkowski, D. (Eds.) *Gilles Deleuze and
     the Theater of Philosophy*. Routledge, 1994, pp. 229-261.

20   Deleuze, G. 1981, *op cit*. p. 19, translation in Polan, D. *op cit*. p. 238.

21   Deleuze, G. 1981, *op cit*. p. 27, translation in Smith, D. 'Deleuze's Theory of
     Sensation: Overcoming Kant's Duality' in Patton, P. (Ed.) *Deleuze: A Critical*

Reader. Blackwell, 1996. Here Deleuze is again drawing a parallel between Bacon and Cézanne.

22 A short but useful discussion of Bacon by Deleuze, in English, can be found in 'Portraits in Extremis' by Jonathan Keates with a text by Gilles Deleuze in *The Magazine of Franco Maria Ricci*. 1985, pp. 45-60.

23 Deleuze, G. and Guattari, F. *What is Philosophy?* Athlone Press, 1994, pp. 166-7.

24 Deleuze, G. *Difference and Repetition*. Athlone Press, 1994, pp. 56-7.

25 Deleuze, G. and Guattari, F. 1994, *op cit*. p. 167.

26 *Ibid*. p. 176.

27 *Ibid*. p. 175.

28 Deleuze, G. 1981, *op cit*. p. 66. The notion of painting as 'operative' is used throughout the volume. Here Deleuze talks about Bacon's 'diagram' of colour being '*l'ensemble opératoire des traits et des taches*' (an operative group of lines and marks).

29 'Intellectuals and Power: A Conversation between Michel Foucault and Gilles Deleuze' in Foucault, M. *Language, Counter-Memory, Practice*. Donald F. Bouchard (Ed.) Cornell University Press, 1977, p. 208. See also: Brian Massumi's foreword to Deleuze, G. and Guattari, F. 1988, *op cit*. p. *xv*.

30 Sylvester, D. *op cit*. p. 92.

31 *Ibid*. pp. 92 & 94.

32 *Ibid*. p. 96.

After Adorno: Art, Autonomy, and Critique

John Roberts

Abstract

This chapter deals with the issue of art's autonomy in the wake of the crisis of high modernism and the rise of post modernism. Focusing on Adorno's aesthetic theory, I look at how under modernity anti-art and art's autonomy are indivisible aspects of art's 'going on'. For in order to sustain itself, art must renew its autonomy through negating its autonomy. This argument is examined through an analysis of some aspects of contemporary practice and the debate on popular culture. In conclusion I defend the dialectical implications of Adorno's writing against both his postmodern critics and a recent Adornian philosophical aesthetics or New Aestheticism.

In conversation with two artist friends recently they both declared that Adorno was a far more serious and productive guide to their practices than any other philosopher or aesthetician. Given their work and histories as artists - one had lived through the period of conceptual art and had been won over briefly to its arguments, the other emerged out of its ruins - this was a surprise. Like many artists in the late seventies and early eighties both had fallen under the sway of Walter Benjamin, and were convinced, in their respective ways, that the dissolution of the category of Art into the forms of modern technology and everyday life was a good thing. Indeed both artists were proselytisers for photography and its powers of social reference and communality. Discussions of art's autonomy were not on their check list of priorities. In fact, if autonomy was discussed or thought of at all it was denounced as a bourgeois category. Autonomy was what Clement Greenberg and modernist painters believed in, and the bane of all materialist art criticism. It was not what serious post-conceptualist artists, armed with the 'critique of representation' and theories of the social production of art, should be worrying about.

Today, however, the confidence of their admonitions has diminished considerably. Where there was a commitment to the possibility of a non-specialist audience for art, and a consideration of art's social role in their thinking, now there is a turn to the space and time and immanent problems of the artwork itself. The question of autonomy, accordingly, has resurfaced, only now in a setting which is far more sympathetic to its claims.

Why is this so? It is of course highly dubious to credit the work of one author with effecting this kind of change. Yet, since the publication of *Aesthetic Theory* in English in 1984, [1] Adorno's writing has had an extensive influence on the rethinking of the question of autonomy in Anglophone art theory and philosophical aesthetics. Indeed, the views of my two anonymous artists are not that unusual; Adorno's work has undergone a widespread revival of interest, generating by the late 1990s a minor academic industry in Europe and North America. This is because there is an increasing recognition that both the critique and the defence of autonomy have been *undertheorized* since the seventies; and this being so, Adorno's work is well-placed to give a number of powerful reasons why.

The return to Adorno, needs to be seen, therefore, as part of a deeper response to what is perceived as the wider crisis in art and theory in the wake of the institutional demise of American modernism and the successful rise of postmodernism prior to, and out of the ruins of, the collapse of European communism and the current crisis of the left. In fact it is the struggle over the ideological legitimation of postmodernism that has allowed Adorno to find a new critical readership today. For amongst anti-postmodernists Adorno is being read not so much as an élitist defender of high modernism - although of course some do read him in this way - but primarily as the scourge of the false or *premature* democracy of postmodernism. Despite postmodernism's purported attack on élitism its critique of autonomy is judged as having produced little in the way of actual transformative social institutions and collective cultural practice. Since the late seventies the dominant form of postmodernism - critical postmodernism - has become linked with the cultural aspirations of the new middle class, as it reinvents the basis of artistic professionalism out of the struggles of feminism and anti-racism, post-colonial theory and queer theory. The outcome is a convergence in art between the critique of the mass media, social identity, representation and the institutions of art, and new forms of bourgeois social and academic administration.

This influence of this liberal-left agenda within some of the major cultural and academic institutions of our time is seen by many as a progressive historical achievement. Modernism's dedifferentiated, socially abstract subject has been decisively challenged by the cultural impact of subaltern and marginalized subjectivities, irredeemably damaging the case against familiar conservative accusations of the 'lowering of standards'. But, if postmodernism is in a position of some strength against the critics of multiculturalism and 'anti-aestheticism', it is extremely vulnerable when its claims to cultural emancipation are examined in the light of the narrow class composition of its social base. Just as postmodernism's critique of the avant-garde presents insuperable problems once art's negation of tradition is abandoned for the moral authority of social and political intervention.

Indeed, it is the dissolution of the normative basis of modern art's negation of tradition that has generated the renewed interest in Adorno. For Adorno's defence of autonomy is based on the fundamental premise that art's continued critical potential rests on its resistance to the authority of tradition, whether or not this tradition speaks in the name of social emancipation and enlightenment. Without this process of renewal the transmission of value and meaning in art becomes subject to the positivity of an external, self-legitimating authority and the pieties of 'commitment'. In short, art defines itself through its received codes and protocols, denying the demands of the present in the name of the securities of the past.

Given this, Adorno's defence of autonomy is not to be confused with the transcendental separation of art from its social base or traditional aesthetic conservativism. Rather, autonomy is the name given to the process of formal and cognitive self-criticism which art must undergo in order to constitute the conditions of its *very possibility and emergence*. In a world which continually reduces the discursive and non-discursive complexities of art to the reconciliations of entertainment, fashion and (recently) social and cultural theory, this self-criticism is an ethical necessity.

The postmodern critique of autonomy, then, confuses the process of self-criticism with simplistic modernist claims of formal development or advance in art. Accordingly, it fails to scrutinise its own academic and idealist conditions of production and reception, insisting that the technological dissolution of art into everyday life claimed by much contemporary practice makes the intimacy between formal values and ethics historically redundant. But this misunderstanding of autonomy is not confined to Adorno's postmodern critics. A number of Adorno's defenders are themselves guilty of traducing its dialectical content. The move 'back to' to Adorno has also generated a proto-conservative reading of autonomy, in which postmodernism is attacked without any proper critical consideration of the expanded social base of the bourgeois institutions of art in the 1980s and 1990s and the critical content of the art since conceptualism.

As such, fifteen years after the publication of *Aesthetic Theory*, Adorno's new readership stands at the centre of a number of competing critiques of postmodernism. In the following I examine the claims of these positions in the ongoing debate on postmodernism and art, as the basis for an assessment of the possibility of Adorno's continuing relevance for philosophical aesthetics and art theory.

It is possible to divide contemporary Adornian studies into five main categories:

1   The dialogic critics of Adorno, as in the school of post-60s German Critical Theory, specifically, Jürgen Habermas and Albrecht Wellmer; [2]

2   Peter Bürger's Brechtian critique of Adorno's aesthetic autonomy as a retreat from social praxis; [3]

3   The philosophical defenders of Adorno as a radical aesthete, as in the writing of philosophers J. M. Bernstein, Andrew Bowie, and the recent translator of the new edition of *Aesthetic Theory*, Robert Hullot-Kentor; [4]

4   The anti-Habermasian interpretation of Adorno as the great theorist of 'totality' and 'reification', as in Fredric Jameson; [5] and

5   The defenders of Adorno as the dialectical theorist of autonomy, as in the philosophical aesthetics of Lambert Zuidervaart and Peter Osborne. [6]

Category 1 has affinities with the postmodern critique of Adorno and autonomy, despite its antipathy to postmodernism as a cultural category and philosophical phenomenon.

Both Habermas and Wellmer argue that Adorno's defence of autonomy is falsely opposed to instrumental rationality, and therefore judge that the work of art is overdetermined as a model of truth. By insisting on autonomy as the basis of artistic value, Adorno opens up an irreconcilable gap between the artwork and socially shared knowledge and social transformation. In sum, Adorno's aesthetic theory for Habermas and Wellmer lacks any proper or reasonable dialogic content. This is because Adorno's hieratic model of reification reduces the conversational and communicative potential of the artwork to a bare minimum. In fact, Adorno always opposes the 'expressive' truth of the artwork to its socially communicative function. The upshot of this being that Adorno has no interest in how people actually experience and use works of art, how their content is mediated *in* everyday life. Art, insist Habermas and Wellmer, does not signify by virtue of its 'intrinsic' expressiveness, but through the intersubjective agency of a given discursive community of reception.

For Bürger, in Category 2, this objection to Adorno's would-be indifference to art's discursive functions, forms an explicit political defence of art as social praxis. Whereas Habermas and Wellmer reclaim the notion of art's autonomy under a quasi-Kantian transcendental reason, Bürger dispenses with the dialectics of autonomy altogether. This is based on what Bürger sees as Adorno's wilful historical misrepresentation of the role and function of the avant-garde. By subsuming the post-autonomous artistic claims of the original revolutionary Soviet and German avant-garde under the critical model of the modern neo-avant-garde, Adorno fails to recognise the qualitatively distinctive moment of the original: namely, that it broke with the high-cultural institutions of art. Adorno's model of autonomy simply continues the death-throes of art's aesthetic and esoteric specialization.

Wellmer's and Habermas's model has had a certain amount of influence, particularly within feminist cultural criticism, which sees Adorno's theory of autonomy as modelled on the repression of bodily pleasures and women's everyday experience. By insisting on modernism as the disaffirmation of sensual pleasure Adorno inherits the iconophobic rationalization of art in post-Platonic philosophy. The Kantian and Hegelian scepticism about sensible form becomes the fear of sensuality as a loss of intellectual control, and as such an unconscious fear of bodily pleasure. However, as Sabine Wilke and Heidi Schlipphacke, argue, this is not because Adorno's modernism allows no place for sensuality and non-disaffirmative pleasures (Adorno is keen on the somatic playfulness of the circus for instance), but that bodily pleasures and sexual difference are left behind 'on the trajectory towards aesthetic autonomy.' [7] Wilke and Schlipphacke note that this repression is there at the very beginning of *Aesthetic Theory*, when Adorno defines autonomy in emphatic Hegelian terms as a parting of the ways from bodily determination. With Romanticism 'art emancipated itself from cuisine and pornography, an emancipation that has become irrevocable.' [8]

In contrast to categories 1 and 2, Bernstein and Bowie in Category 3, defend Adorno's dialectic of enlightenment against what is judged to be the sanguine and conciliatory critique of modernity in the dialogic model of art and the premature dissolution of art into everyday life in Bürger.

In this respect this position sets out to redefine the redemptive content of Adorno's claim for art's autonomy. In Adorno, the defence of autonomy is construed ontologically as first and foremost a defence of aesthetic semblance or illusion. By this Adorno means that it is the artefactual character of the artwork that secures its autonomy, because it is the artefactual character of art which establishes the possibility of aesthetic rationality overcoming instrumental rationality. As socialised, non-coercive labour, or purposeless purposiveness in the language of Kant, the artwork's fabricated uselessness is able to recall for the viewer the human, non-instrumental purpose of production. Famously this notion of aesthetic form as a redemption of alienated labour becomes a defence of what Adorno calls the process of mimesis internal to the autonomous artwork: its capacity to sustain a relationship of non-instrumental affinity between subject and object. Autonomous artworks, in this sense, both preserve and present the possibility of other kinds of experience. As Bernstein puts it:

the question of aesthetic semblance is the question of the possibility of possibility, of a conception of possible experience that transcends what is now taken to be the parameters of possible experience. [9]

From this perspective, Bernstein, Bowie and other radical aesthetes draw two significant conclusions from the notion of art as the enactment of a promise, which set them off sharply from the dialogic critics of Adorno. The promise of happiness is separate from the mere satisfaction of desire or bodily pleasure - hence the criticisms of the kind made by Wilke and Schlipphacke are misplaced; and that particular things can be unsubsumable under conceptual categories and yet remain sources of meaning. As a consequence it is the transcendent promise of the reconciliation between sensuality and spirituality in the autonomous artwork, which grounds the truth-claims of art.

Category 4 is similarly preoccupied with the transcendent promise of the artwork. But for Fredric Jameson what is of general concern is how this promise has come into its own again in an historical period of continued stalled social and political transformation. Whereas in the 1970s in the age of national liberation, high-levels of class struggle, and radical cultural transformation, Adorno's promise was seen as an 'encumbrance' and 'embarrassment', [10] today it keeps alive the untruth of capitalist rationality and freedom. This is because the very historical possibility of the autonomous artwork is what exposes the false totality of capitalist production. Through a deeper commitment to aesthetic truth as the non-negotiable source of dereification and disalienation, Adorno demonstrates that aesthetic theory is never *merely* aesthetic. What is of paramount significance in Adorno for Jameson, therefore, is that all aesthetic questions are taken to be fundamentally historical ones. But, as a consequence of this, Jameson refrains from making actual judgements about modernist works themselves; this is because it is not so much the specific content of Adorno's defence of various kinds of modernist art that counts, but the implications of aesthetic praxis as redemption as a whole. The outcome is a reticence and, even, guardedness about what constitutes the content and boundaries of autonomous art today. Indeed, there is a clear tendency in both the philosophical aesthetics of Category 3, and Jameson's position, to evacuate the problems and contradictions of contemporary art practice for the promise of the promise itself. This is the result in Jameson, as in Bernstein and Bowie, of an undialectical interpretation of the *social* content of Adorno's concept of autonomy.

What distinguishes Adorno's theory of autonomy from the early Romantics, the neo-conservative New Criticism of the 1950s, and Greenbergian modernists, is that art is seen simultaneously as socially determined *and* autonomous. Or rather, the autonomy of the art object is something which is produced out of the social relations which constitute the institution of art itself. It is not something which is produced immanently out of the object and therefore transmittable as a particular 'style' or 'look'. This means that autonomy is the practical and theoretical outcome of the contradiction between the artwork's exchange value and use-value. Because of the perpetual threat of the loss of the artwork's use-value, art is continually propelled by its own conditions of alienation to find aesthetic strategies which might resist or obviate this process of critical and aesthetic dissolution - the history of the 'new' in modernism derives from the resistance of art to its exchange value. But, at the same time, under capitalism art derives its social identity and value from this process. Thus authentic modern art acquires identity and value in a double movement of negation and self-negation: art achieves visibility through positioning itself in relation to the prevailing norms, interests and protocols of the market and intellectual academy. But once the work achieves institutional and market visibility, the artist is forced to resist the work's own subsumption under a new set of norms if he or she values the thing that defined the work's initial moment of production: its critical difference or aesthetic 'otherness'. For once the value of the new work is institutionally established, the work finds itself part of a new set of prevailing norms and protocols. The exchange value of the artwork, therefore, operates as a kind of 'fiction': artists seek to transform the normative values of the market and the critical academy in their own image, but in the interests of escaping from these values and self-image. That is, the 'fiction' of autonomy has to be dismantled by the artist if the pursuit of autonomy is to be able to continue to prosecute art's failure to realise its freedom from social dependency. Art's autonomy is *necessarily dependent* on the alienated conditions of its realization, because it is through art's connection to the 'unresolved antagonisms' of reality that the social content of autonomy is generated. Commodification, then, locks art into an impossible logic: art can only renew itself through undermining or disrupting those qualities that bring it into being. Yet if this logic is impossible, for Adorno it is necessary and inescapable under current relations of production, because, paradoxically, it is this logic which sustains the possibility of art's (and human) freedom. In this sense the possibility of art's autonomy is *socially* driven.

This expansive notion of autonomy is something that is explored in detail in the dialectical theory of autonomy in Category 5, particularly in the work of Lambert Zuidervaart and Peter Osborne.

What these writers insist on - which I concur with - is the need for a sharper reintegration of the truth of autonomy into the cultural and social experience of recent art and postmodernism. That is, they call for a development of autonomy away from its recent grounding in modernist painting and sculpture into the area of new media and their interconnections. For if the value of autonomy rests on its commitment to finding new materials and forms of attention for the 'unresolved antagonisms' of social experience, then this must of necessity be expanded into an analysis of the problems which confront the art of the present, without recourse to nostalgia or moralism. Without the establishment of the link between the expanded means and materials of the art of the last thirty years and the problem of autonomy, aesthetic value is forced back into a conservative reading of the modern. In this way Adorno's dialectics must be brought to bear on Adorno's categories themselves, as a recognition of the historicity of autonomy itself.

Importantly, this means transforming the relationship between high-art and popular culture in Adorno's aesthetic theory. For it is the would-be fixture of this binary opposition between 'high' and 'low' that identifies the current historical limits of Adorno's defence of autonomy and that of his contemporary philosophical defenders, who tend to see the art of the last thirty years as a falling away from the sensual achievements of modernism. [11] The failure to acknowledge the expanded social content of autonomy on the part of these defenders is invariably the result of their condescension, or outright hostility, towards mass culture and popular culture. Yet the expanded content of the art of the last thirty years is incomprehensible without a recognition of how the 'low' has challenged and reconfigured the 'high'. But, breaking with this condescension towards the popular is not an invitation to dissolve the 'high' *into* the 'low', as in the populist tendencies of postmodernism. Rather, it allows the possibility of a dialectics of 'high' *and* 'low': that is, it re-establishes the opposition between 'high' and 'low' in the light of the contradictions inherent in *both* terms. And this, of course, is something that Adorno himself was highly sensitive to, and which first preoccupied him in the 1930s, even if his judgement on the 'low' was essentially sceptical.

Adorno's antipathy to mass culture is notorious and much criticised. This is based on his view that although high-art or autonomous art, and mass culture or dependent art, are both commodities, dependent artworks are incapable of generating sustainable critical reflection on the part of the spectator and reader. Rather, mass culture offers compensatory forms of libidinal gratification, and as such, functions overall as a form of social repression. The pleasures of mass culture negate the promise of happiness of autonomous art. Yet when Adorno actually talks about the 'high' and the 'low' in *Aesthetic Theory*, the 'high' refers to the interrelations between autonomy and dependency, of which autonomy is the dominant term. Similarly, Adorno is well aware that in mass culture there are moments of autonomy. As he was to say in a letter to Benjamin on March 18, 1936, 'If you defend the *kitsch* film against the "quality" film, no one can be more in agreement with you than I am; but *l'art pour l'art* is just as much in need of a defence.' [12] As such it is important to stress that Adorno does not identify mass culture *with* the culture industry; the culture industry is what capitalism does to mass culture. But two things interconnect to make his judgements about modern mass culture utterly marginal in his aesthetic theory: his totalizing view of the reification of mass experience; and as such his overwhelming commitment to analyzing mass culture from the standpoint of autonomous art. Thus, no popular art quite meets the highest standards of the best autonomous art, and the best of autonomous art is always compelled to preserve its boundaries against the encroachments of aesthetic dependency.

In this respect, like Category 2, Category 5 distances itself from autonomy as a precondition of the evaluation of all art. As with Bürger - and Habermas and Wellmer - the dialectical theory of autonomy accepts that the truth of autonomy is not the ultimate criterion of art's social significance. Indeed, this conclusion is self-evident in a culture where traditional modernist forms of autonomy no longer provide any moral or political challenge to the effects of reification. Just as the pleasures of mass culture and popular culture do not have to negate the promise of happiness, but can, as Osborne says, at certain moments, 'heighten the sense of frustration at the broken promise.' [13] As a consequence, it is hard to accept, in Adorno's terms, that autonomous art is any more critically effective than dependent art when certain products of mass culture can subvert the conventions of the traditions they operate within and disclose, on occasions, radical aspirations.

On this basis the debate on the dialectical content of autonomy is an attack on Adorno's traditional concern for normative evaluation. Irrespective of their 'levels' of 'autonomy' or 'social dependency' all works of art demonstrate a social function. However, unlike Bürger and the postmodernists, to accept the multiple and variegated functions and forms of reception of artworks does not thereby mean accepting the abandonment of normativity altogether - the postmodernist syndrome of defining art as popular culture and popular culture as art. Rather, what is required is a more differentiated account of art's standards and criteria of evaluation, what Zuidevaart calls a 'complex normativity'. [14] This complex normativity might include not only 'technical excellence, formal depth, aesthetic expressiveness' (attributes conventionally associated with modernism) but also 'social scope, potential effectiveness and historical truth'. 'Rarely would a particular work meet all these norms, nor would very many works display exceptional merit with respect to every norm that they do meet.' [15] By this, Zuidevaart means that the supposedly élitist concern with autonomy allows us to rethink the dynamics of popular pleasure and technological development in art, at the same time as the dynamics of popular pleasure and technological development in art can allow us to rethink the limits and content of autonomy. Indeed normativity is unavoidable once we accept that the critique of the category of art remains inseparable from the continuing conditions of art's possibility.

Osborne adopts a similar position to this. But, in contrast to Zuidervaart, he is far more forceful in arguing that the implications of this dialectic are there latent in Adorno's work itself. As he says:

Adorno's own analysis suggests another, far more productive approach (to the question of autonomy): *namely, to lay bare the structure of the dialectic of the dependent and the autonomous within dependent art, and to comprehend it through its opposition to autonomous art, as a distinctive part of a larger cultural whole.* [16]

This insistence on the solution to the problem of autonomy lying in the transformation of Adorno's categories themselves is held, rightly, by Osborne to be a political decision. To defend autonomy in the spirit of Adorno as an historical and interrelational concept is to resist those who would judge negation and the critique of tradition in art to be dead and buried. In this respect the continuing importance of Adorno lies in how his concept of autonomy incorporates the irreconcilability of art to its own alienated conditions and fate into the conditions of its own possibility. The idea, therefore, that art can resolve these conditions by claiming allegiance to a singular aesthetic tradition or by dissolving itself *into* everyday life, is an avoidance of the realities of art's alienation, whether these forms of reconciliation are offered in the name of cultural democracy or not. Hence the fundamental problem with Bürger's, Habermas's and Wellmer's models - and postmodernism as a whole - is that in their various ways they fail to acknowledge the violence and misrepresentation which underwrite art's mediation of cultural and social division. As such, in the case of Habermas, Wellmer and the postmodernists, they assume far too easy an incorporation of the artwork into the principles of communicative rationality, when human suffering and reification are always threatening to dissolve this rationality into incoherence, bad faith and sentiment. Indeed the rejection of all forms of aesthetic and social compensation in Adorno's theory of autonomy is designed not in order to foreclose all possible communication, but to render the truth of art as existentially and formally continuous *with* the effects of alienation and reification. By defending a form of autonomy which is constituted through the negation of tradition the irreconcilability of art is coextensive with the irreconcilability of the subject's consciousness of being-in-the-world.

Adorno's legacy, then, needs to be defended against those who would abandon normativity for *shallow* defences of the 'popular' and art's basis in communal discursivity, and all the political substitutionalism that inevitably comes with such positions. However, at the same time, it needs to be recognised that the theoretical resources in Adorno for *sustaining* the social content of autonomy, are highly attenuated, opening up room for misunderstanding and false departures, as in the writing of the Adornian philosophical aesthetes. This is not least because Adorno's notional recognition of the 'autonomous' in the 'dependent' and the 'dependent' in the 'autonomous' leaves the social character of his concept of autonomy highly ambiguous.

Viewed from this perspective, one of the problems with Adorno's writing for his philosophical aesthetic defenders is how to position the claims of anti-art in relation to the critique of tradition, particularly in the light of the most important art of the last thirty years, which has systematically expanded the forms and meanings of aesthetic experience through the strategies of anti-art.

The moment of anti-art for Adorno is determinate for the renewal of art's autonomy; in order to distinguish itself from what has *become* aesthetic, art is forced to expand into, or reclaim non-aesthetic, experiences, forms or practices, (popular and discursive modes of attention, the ready made, the textual, etc.). But for Adorno this is heavily qualified by his view that such moves always threaten to dissolve the artwork back *into* the real and the everyday. This leads him to attack the aesthetics of the ready-made and to devalue photography. The radical aesthetes of Category 3, tend to follow this line, settling for the formal evaluations of Adorno's misjudged conclusions, rather than the dialectical implications of his argument. Consequently, they maintain that Adorno's critical potential today lies in his resistance to the dissolution of the artefactual and sensual base of artistic practice. But if this critique is pursued in order to draw attention to the false democracy of the 'popular' and anti-form, etc., - critical postmodernism is uppermost in their minds - it also threatens to disengage autonomy from Adorno's hermeneutical privileging of the 'new' out of anti-art. [17] If the 'new' in art is the constitution of art's autonomy through the determinate negation of tradition, then the impulse of anti-art is *integral* to what has previously established itself as autonomous, and therefore essential to the social content of autonomy. Without this moment of negation autonomy in art degenerates into a confirmation of tradition and the present, meaning that, anti-art is a transgression that autonomy must undergo in order to reconstitute itself. [18] Accordingly, one of the reasons that there is a close identification between autonomy and the *aesthetics* of modernism in work of the writers in Category 3, is that philosophical aesthetics takes the superseded and conventionalized forms of anti-art in modernism as its guide to contemporary practice, losing the *positional logic* of anti-art in the pursuit of art's autonomy. In this sense it is the positional logic of anti-art which drives the social content of art's autonomy. In this way the ambiguity of Adorno's legacy tends to be exacerbated by this kind of philosophical aesthetics, because it treats the concept of autonomy as an abstract philosophical postulate, and not as something determined by the prevailing conditions of art's autonomy.

Adorno's concept of autonomy, then, generates two interconnected problems for its radical aesthete defenders:

• in the interests of stabilising aesthetic quality and high-culture's negation of mass culture it weakens the moment of anti-art within art's pursuit of autonomy; and

• in order to distinguish the authenticity of autonomy in art it represses the transcendent moment of autonomy immanent to all forms of culture.

This leaves his defenders with very little to use aesthetically when coming to understand the art of the recent past and the massive expansion and diversification of popular cultures in the 1980s and 1990s. By identifying autonomy with tired modernist protocols and by defending an implausible account of ideology and popular culture - popular culture as fundamentally antithetical to the fulfilment of human needs - the radical aesthetes dissolve autonomy into a defensive aestheticism. [19] In this respect the dialectical critics of autonomy are correct: the interrelations between autonomy and mass culture are dead in the water unless retheorized as part of the critical expansion of art's normativity. By expanding the content of normativity the opposition between modernism/anti-reification and mass culture/reification is revealed to be no longer functional as a source of absolute value - if ever it was. But, if the dialectical theorists of autonomy correctly relativize the issue of reification, there is, similarly, little sense what this might actually mean in terms of the problems of contemporary art and culture. Osborne's notion of the 'critical potential of mass culture', [20] is frustratingly vague.

It is not of course the job of philosophy to answer such questions; philosophy cannot predict or legislate the content of art's autonomy. However, what it can and should do is clarify the conditions for a defence of the social content of autonomy against its premature aestheticization or dissolution. Hence, the dismantling of the opposition between a high modernist singular normativity and a dependent popular culture, means little unless questions of value, meaning and pleasure are based on a theory of artistic subjectivity and spectatorship which adequately represent contemporary transformations in art and culture.

The central problem with the philosophical aesthetes' defence of a version of the traditional modernist subject and spectator is, as I have stressed, its lack of cultural differentiation. What demands our attention, therefore, if we are to establish a workable notion of autonomy is the need to connect the expanded social and aesthetic conditions of art since the 1960s to a theory of negation in art - or anti-art - that does not merely reproduce or reverse the antinomy between 'high' and 'low'. By this I mean that if the concept of autonomy is no longer able to sustain its negative logic through modernism's classical forms of distantiation it requires an aesthetic subject/producer which derives its critical agency from the relations *between* an expanded notion of social identity and form in art and the exclusions and aporias of social and cultural division. In other words, an adequate notion of autonomy is to be derived from the aesthetic subject/producer's mediation of the interrelations of 'high' and 'low', and not merely from their abstract conjunction.

Consequently, the concept of 'complex normativity' becomes clearer if we take the contemporary incorporation of popular modes of attention into the expanded social categories of art as a response to modernist 'expressiveness', as itself divided. The significance of the 'relativization of reification' for a complex normativity is not that it allows art to switch to the popular from the demands of critical distance, but that art's critical functions are structured within an understanding of the popular as both pleasurable *and* alienated. By stressing that popular modes of attention and pleasures define a shared space in which both 'high' and 'low' position themselves in late capitalist culture, the demands of autonomy are situated as internal to the determinations of dependency. Popular forms of attention are not so much the 'other' of authentic aesthetic life, but the dominant space out of which aesthetic pleasures and values are formed and struggled over.

From this perspective the experience of the aesthetic subject/producer is opened up to the pleasures of popular culture and mass culture *without condescension*, which is a significantly different proposition from Adorno's occasional embrace of popular pleasures as a kind of healthy antidote to middle-brow taste. In this way embodied popular pleasures are enjoyed precisely because they refuse to give unqualified assent to the supposed enlightened pleasures of high-culture. However, this refusal of assent does not imply that the taking of such pleasures is a negation of high-culture or that such pleasures are identifiable with an undiscriminating cultural pluralism. On this understanding of the aesthetic subject the taking of pleasures from the popular is not to be confused with the postmodern notion of the popular consumer. Rather, the aesthetic subject takes pleasure from the popular knowing such pleasures *to be* alienated. This is an important epistemological difference, for it reveals something significant that neither the Adornian philosophical aesthetes nor postmodernists take much notice of about the conditions of modern culture: that the pleasures taken from popular culture and high culture are mutually unstable for would-be popular consumers and 'aesthetes' alike - even if this instability is in the final analysis subject to the wider constraints of class division, and therefore unstable in uneven ways. But the important point is that the taking of such pleasures is itself a process of internal division and dissent, for, there is no such thing as the uncultured and unfeeling popular consumer - everybody comes to popular culture and to a work of art with some knowledge and powers of discrimination whatever their educational and cultural accomplishments. And, similarly, this is precisely the point about the cultural limitations inherent in the position of the aesthete, for the aesthete is no less alienated than the popular cultural consumer - alienated by his or her own fantasy of aesthetic control. So, just as popular modes of attention are themselves internally differentiated under the demands of aesthetic discrimination, the aesthete's would-be disinterested pleasures are the constant, repressive reminder of the embodied and subaltern pleasures of the popular.

Thus, what the concept of complex normativity is able to establish is that both works of autonomous art (high culture) and the products of popular culture share a *common* space of reification and dereification. This allows us to theorize artistic production and reception without recourse to a simplistic model of high culture as the protection of a single normativity and low culture as the degradation of normativity - of one (higher) form of autonomy subsuming another. Indeed the idea of the aesthete as the defender of a normative autonomy and the popular consumer as the undifferentiated consumer of mass culture is utterly regressive. Consequently, the aesthetic subject/producer who acknowledges the dependency in autonomy and moments of autonomy in dependency, might be said to be extending the implications of Adorno's aesthetic theory, but crucially, from within a critical space where cultural alienation is treated as complex and internal to both terms. For the overwhelming problem with the Adornian philosophical aesthetes, is that the conflicts of aesthetic experience are not viewed as the result of the actual and symbolic violence internal to high culture *and* popular culture.

To link the question of aesthetics to symbolic violence is to make clear what connects the debate on art and the popular to what remains of importance in Adorno's writing on autonomy: the fact that the internal and external divisions of autonomy and mass culture are only comprehensible within a *continuum* of actual or symbolic violence. To analyse autonomy and dependency, in terms of the actual and symbolic violence perpetrated against works of art by the culture industry and aestheticism, and in terms of the symbolic violence internal to the social logic of art's autonomy, is to see how modern art's internal history and external relations with mass culture in the 20th century exist in a continuum of destruction and derogation. What this discloses, importantly, is how symbolic and actual violence constitute the ontological condition of art's production and reception under capitalism. Thus to acknowledge the incorporation of the moment of anti-art into art in terms of the irreconcilability of art's being-in-the-world is to foreground the philosophical and cultural intimacy between negation (of identity) with violence. The logic of art's autonomy is its process of internal disidentification in the face of art's external derogation.

Theories of aesthetics, however, are largely concerned with dissolving art's interpresence with symbolic and actual violence. As Paul de Man puts it in his critique of aesthetic ideology: 'the *aesthetic* is not a separate category but a principle of articulation between various known categories, and modes of cognition.' [21] But, an acceptance of this separation is what leads to the culturally undifferentiated aesthete and to the abandonment of a complex normativity and the exigencies of anti-art. The self-divided aesthetic subject, however, challenges this loss of differentiation, insofar as it restores an active recognition and critique of the structural violence internal and external to both the production and reception of art and popular culture. [22] The question of 'complex normativity' as the relativization of reification, therefore, remains incoherent if it does not make visible how the artist and spectator are now situated in a contested space between the modes of attention of popular culture and their critique. It is out of this space between the identification and disidentification of these modes that the contemporary conditions of a 'complex normativity' are currently being produced. [23]

The threat to art's autonomy is immanent to the social conditions of art's existence. But it is the social conditions of art's production and reception which bring the autonomy of the artwork (its challenge to the instrumentalities of market and academy) into being. Autonomous art remains authentically autonomous inasmuch as the conditions of its production recognise this and resist its instrumental and extra-artistic logic. Adorno's expressive model in *Aesthetic Theory*, is as I have outlined, based on this. But Adorno is unable to develop this because the social content of autonomy is prematurely separated from the negation of autonomy within autonomy - the moment of anti-art. He is unable to see - or trust fully - anti-art as the means by which autonomy is able to mediate art's futural condition and the relations between art and knowledge. This might be described as the moment of 'realism' in art's autonomy, the moment which grounds the dynamic movement of autonomy's social content. Adorno's philosophical followers, however, dissolve this movement, by resolving the issue of autonomy in terms of the defence of a single normativity - against what they see as the loss of all normativity in postmodernism. In this, the philosophical defence of autonomy as the negation of aesthetic tradition and protocol remains imperative in the face of the aggressive rejection of normativity in postmodern cultural studies and the positivization of negation in philosophical aesthetics. But the dialectical defence of autonomy is no source of artistic value. It is only the practices and criticism of art that is able to open up the social content of autonomy. Philosophy's job is to underwrite that possibility, not to substitute itself for that possibility.

References and notes

1   Adorno, Theodor W. [1970] 1984, *Aesthetic Theory*. (Transl. C. Lenhardt)
    London: Routledge & Kegan Paul.

2   Habermas, Jürgen. [1985] 'Questions and Counterquestions' in *Habermas
    and Modernity*, (Ed. and introduced by Richard J. Bernstein), Cambridge:
    Polity Press; *idem*. [1986] *Autonomy and Solidarity*. (Ed. and introduced by
    Peter Dews) London: Verso; and Wellmer, Albrecht. 'Reason, Utopia and the
    Dialectic of Enlightenment', in Bernstein, Richard J. (Ed) [1985] *ibid.*

3   Bürger, Peter. (1974) [1984] *The Theory of the Avant-Garde*. London and
    Minnesota: University of Minnesota Press. It is worth pointing out that
    Bürger's Brechtianism in *The Theory of the Avant-Garde*, was one of the
    principal sources of reception of Adorno on the left in the Anglo-American
    academy until the publication of *Aesthetic Theory*.

4   Bernstein, Jay M. [1992] *The Fate of Art: Aesthetic Alienation from Kant to
    Derrida and Adorno*. Cambridge: Polity Press; Bowie, Andrew. [1990]
    Aesthetics and Subjectivity: from Kant to Nietzsche. Manchester:
    Manchester University Press; and Hullot-Kentor, Robert. [1997] 'Translator's
    Note', in *Theodor W. Adorno, Aesthetic Theory*. London: Athlone Press.

5   Jameson, Fredric. [1990] *Late Marxism: Adorno, or, the Persistence of the
    Dialectic*. London: Verso. Of the five categories that I have proposed
    Jameson's has the least functional value, insofar as his defence of Adorno in
    Late Marxism, is mainly pedagogic. He doesn't elaborate why Adorno's
    concept of autonomy has value today. This may have something to do with
    the fact that his engagement with contemporary culture is within comparative
    literature and architecture and not within the visual arts, where the question
    of autonomy has immediate and continuing valency.

6   Zuidervaart, Lambert. [1991] *Adorno's Aesthetic Theory: The Redemption of
    Illusion*. Cambridge Massachusetts: MIT; Osborne, Peter. [1989] 'Aesthetic
    Autonomy and the Crisis of Theory: Greenberg, Adorno and the Problem of
    Postmodernism in the Visual Arts', in *New Formations*, No 9, Winter; and
    idem. [1989] 'Torn Halves: The Dialectics of a Cultural Dichotomy', *News
    From Nowhere*, No 7 Winter.

7   Wilke, Sabine and Schlipphacke, Heidi. [1997] 'Construction of a Gendered Subject: A Feminist Reading of Adorno's *Aesthetic Theory*', in Tom Huhn and Lambert Zuidervaart, (Eds.) *The Semblance of Subjectivity: Essays in Adorno's Aesthetic Theory*. Massachusetts: MIT.

8   Adorno, Theodor W. (1970) [1984] *op. cit.* p. 18.

9   Bernstein, Jay M. [1997] 'Why Rescue Semblance? Metaphysical Experience and the Possibility of Ethics', in Tom Huhn and Lambert Zuidervaart, (Eds.) *The Semblance of Subjectivity: Adorno's Aesthetic Theory*. Massachusetts: MIT p. 198.

10 Jameson, Fredric. [1990] *Late Marxism: Adorno, or, the Persistence of the Dialectic*. London: Verso, p. 5.

11 See for example, Clark, T. J. [1999] *Farewell to an Idea: Episodes from a History of Modernism*. Yale, Yale University Press.

12 Adorno, T. (1936) in Bloch, Ernst. *et al*, [1977] *Aesthetics and Politics*. London: NLB, p. 122.

13 Osborne, Peter. [1989] 'Torn Halves: The Dialectics of a Cultural Dichotomy', *News From Nowhere*, No 7 Winter, p. 60.

14 Zuidervaart, Lambert. [1991] *Adorno's Aesthetic Theory: The Redemption of Illusion*. Cambridge Massachusetts: MIT, p. 241.

15 *Ibid.* p. 246.

16 Osborne, P. [1989] *op. cit.* p. 58.

17 Bernstein, Jay. M. [1997] 'Against Voluptuous Bodies', *New Left Review*, No 225

18 For a discussion of this issue see Martin, forthcoming 2000. Martin, Stewart. 'Autonomy and Anti-Art: Adorno's Concept of Avant-Garde Art', *Constellations*, New York.

19   Bowie, Andrew. [1997] 'Confessions of a "New Aesthete"', *New Left Review*, No 225.

20   Osborne, P. [1989] *op. cit.* p. 60.

21   De Man, Paul. [1984] 'Aesthetic Formalization in Kleist', *The Rhetoric of Romanticism*. New York: Columbia University Press, pp. 264-265.

22   One way of mediating this relationship between symbolic and actual violence and the self-divided aesthetic subject might be through the concept of the philistine. See Beech, Dave and Roberts, John. [1996] 'Spectres of the Aesthetic', *New Left Review*, No 218; and *idem*. [1998] 'Tolerating Impurities: An Ontology, Genealogy and Defence of Philistinism', *New Left Review* No 227.

23   For instance much of the work produced in Britain in the 1990s that now goes under the description of Young British Art, and avant-garde US West Coast art of the 1990s.

Supplementary bibliography

Adorno, Theodor W. (1966) [1973] *Negative Dialectics*. London: Routledge & Kegan Paul.

Osborne, Peter. [1992] 'A Marxism for the Postmodern? Jameson's Adorno', in *New German Critique*, No 56 Spring/Summer.

Watson, Ben. [1998] 'Adorno and Music', *Historical Materialism*, No 2 Summer.

Constant Relatives; Sexing Radical Aesthetics: the case of Barbara Hepworth's abstraction.

Penny Florence

Abstract

It is now possible to rethink what used to be understood as universals. Without this framework, it has been a categorical impossibility for progressive thinkers to deal adequately with the kinds of issues raised in and by aesthetics, especially when it comes to sex. Beginning with a brief survey of current feminist/gender-aware writing on aesthetics, including the collection I am co-editing for the *Women's Philosophy Review*, this paper will discuss the potential of a 'differential' aesthetics. Subjectivity and value will be triangulated with the social in an attempt to pass through the 'logic of the same' to outline an approach to aesthetics that neither denies transcendence nor mystifies it.

> *... intent upon emptiness:*
> *As mute stone*
> *Or as a shadowy hand*
>
> *...Nothing at all you can summon*
> *No-one can show me the place that I seek:*
>
> *...Surpass what I cannot*
> *Survive,*
> *Search out to partake*
> *Of the sleeper's metallic condition*
> *And his burning beginnings.*

From *Skystones*, Pablo Neruda, 1970

Barbara Hepworth and aesthetics have arguably been out of favour for about the same time. There are doubtless many contingent reasons for this. But bringing them into alignment in this way can be productive, not least because neither can be understood without addressing the same areas of thought and experience.

Aesthetics can be a meditation on that place sought by Neruda in the poem above. It is also sought by Hepworth. Of course no commentary can ever actually show it, probably rather less than an artifact can; it is like its unconscious. As such, it is however traceable through its effect, inseparably from its affect. And as such it is deeply political. Cultures have framed ineffability in widely differing approaches and forms; but they all seek to embody it some way. It is universal and essential. By using those two words in the current climate, I have probably sent a signal that will be read as the reverse of what I intend. This problem is at the heart of my chapter.

The issues I want to address here are troublesome, then. It seems that the only position from which to articulate them appears at first to be a conservative or even reactionary one. Questions of value and transcendent form still seem out of kilter with most commentators, apart from those who persist in imagining there was (to them) a golden age 'before theory'. They are either the repressed of much current thinking on aesthetics (or what used to be thought of as aesthetics) or set up as a straw opponent.

A significant underlying problem for the writer who takes on questions of difference of any kind, but especially of sexual difference, is the dominant perception that these matters of value and transcendence necessarily invoke universals as absolutes and that they therefore are set apart from considerations of the sexed or of the culturally specific. [1] They are also identified with philosophical positions that are perceived as no longer tenable. For some, they are the absolute rock on which thinking difference founders. For others, the necessity of thinking difference renders them impossibilities. Any concept of the 'universal' is always already compromised in its neutrality, since it is culturally specific and sometimes demonstrably male. This is as commonly understood by feminists as it is ignored by almost everyone else, although it has until recently meant that the whole concept of the universal was rejected.

Some of the important questions raised in traditional aesthetics thus cannot be approached in what has evolved as a radical frame, while at the same time, more radical analyses remain on the starting line when it comes to sex. Sex is crucial in this because it is still only ever really dealt with on the fundamental level necessary within feminist or gender studies - for example, significant recent commentators on aesthetics such as Terry Eagleton, Frederick Jameson or David Carroll do not seem to see the implications of sexed subjectivity as worth considering at all. [2] Others, such as Paul Crowther, raise gender issues only to dismiss them. [3]

Considerable areas of feminist thinking and practice, on the other hand, are hostile to aesthetics, having taken it that the shift into ideology that occurred in the 1960s necessarily excluded any idea of aesthetic value or of transcendence. [4] For many feminist artists of that time, the association of conventionally feminine with the aesthetic, and specifically with the beautiful, meant that it was irretrievably patriarchal. It was, perhaps, a historically necessary position; it is perhaps thanks at least in part to their work that these questions can now be approached again and in new ways. This has indeed slowly begun to happen since the publication in 1993 of *Aesthetics in Feminist Perspective*, although that book has had far less impact than it deserves. [5] The same is true of the 1995 collection *Feminism and Tradition in Aesthetics*. [6] For example, Hilde Hein, Carolyn Korsmeyer, Iris Marion Young, Peg Brand and Christine Battersby [7] have all addressed what was traditional aesthetics in ways that cannot be assimilated to some retrograde 'new aestheticism'. But this is all quite recent, and, apart from Battersby, primarily by critics not based in England. [8]

The situation sketched in very briefly above is important to understanding why an artist such as Barbara Hepworth has not been particularly examined by feminist or radical cultural analysts. It is very difficult to approach her work without a concept of the universal and of the impact formerly known as 'aesthetic'. Her work is therefore very useful here as an example. Understanding Hepworth requires that understandings of the universal be revisited. But it also requires a philosophy of the body that can both account for sexual difference and for the need to go beyond biologism. Her politics and aesthetics are as easily misread as essentialist as Irigaray's philosophy, which is highly influential in this account, if not unproblematically. [9]

This is clear from the critical response to the attempt to reframe Hepworth exemplified by the collection *Barbara Hepworth Reconsidered*, specifically in a recent essay by Charles Harrison. [10] I should declare at once that I have taken this on partly because I think Harrison refers implicitly to my essay in that collection, even though he cites neither. [11] Whether the reference is actual does not matter. I can only hope that the reader will accept that I do so not to personalise the matter, but because the issue has broad ramifications for rethinking aesthetics (as well as for modernism in general and for Hepworth in particular). It is therefore worth looking into in some detail, and the reader will doubtless focus on the issues. Doing this involves a rhetorical strategy which I find difficult: defending one's position in open debate is generally understood to be necessarily adversarial. 'The oppositional' is now entrenched as a critical mode, however, and has in my view lost all the radical potential it may once have had. [12] The task has changed. My interest is in widening engagement with the questions that feminist philosophers and cultural theorists have elaborated, but that still remain 'othered'. There is clearly work of explication to be done. In this sense I am indebted to Harrison for putting his provisional thoughts on paper - and they are declared as provisional - thereby contributing to clarification and debate.

In his essay Harrison makes an observation about how 'we' now view Hepworth. How far he includes himself in this first person plural is unclear, a symptom perhaps of his provisionality. He comments that, according to this putative collective position, Ben Nicholson's white reliefs could be contrasted with Hepworth's 'Three Forms' of 1935 (Figure 1) in its occlusion of 'all and any trace of biological determinism upon psychological life.' [13] This clearly implies that he finds biological determinism in the approach to Hepworth that he goes on to outline thus:

In contrast, what now seems to distinguish such works as Hepworth's 'Three Forms' in white marble is less its modern-movement austerity than its quasi-metaphorical identity as a trio of individuals conceived in terms of physical touch and containment. This may turn out to be a sentimental assessment of Hepworth's work, and thus one in the end irrelevant to the matter of its aesthetic interest. But however we decide on that issue, modern-movement claims for the universality of abstract art are unlikely now to recover their credibility. [14]

FIGURE 1

'Three Forms', Barbara Hepworth, 1935
Copyright Alan Bowness, Hepworth Estate

There is no necessity that a reading of 'Three Forms' as concerning contiguity involves biological determinism. There is here no necessary opposition to modern-movement austerity, no sentimentality [15], and no assertion of quasi-metaphorical identity with individuals, however conceived. What it does involve however, is precisely a reconceptualisation of the modernist claim to universality it is supposed to render unlikely. The substance of Harrison's objection is sufficiently fundamental and indeed representative to warrant taking point by point.

First the notion of a 'quasi-metaphorical identity with individuals'; my reading of 'Three Forms' places it in tension with a variety of elements: the biographical event of giving birth to triplets, number, particularly the tripartite structure, the exterior-interior problematic of corporeality. All this is offered as an exploration of contiguity, which may be related to feminist theorisations of subjectivity in connectedness. This does not of necessity imply 'a quasi-metaphorical identity with individuals' though I can now see how such a misreading might occur. Birth and death are the extremes of the subject's sense of their separation from or connection with humanity. To relate giving multiple birth to an abstract artist's exploration of such universal concerns - and they are universal - is not to suggest that a sculpture has a metaphorical relation with the actual children. Connection, furthermore, can be as difficult and conflicted as separation. It is not, in the new philosophies, cosy. [16]

Harrison later quotes a letter from Rothko to the New York Times in 1945 to illustrate what he sees as the greater significance of his work over that of Ben Nicholson, and this letter helps locate whence the misunderstanding arises. Rothko wrote:

If previous abstractions paralleled the scientific and objective preoccupations of our times, ours are finding a pictorial equivalent for man's new knowledge and consciousness of his more complex inner self. [17]

Rothko reproduces the familiar division between objective and subjective. Hepworth did not. An argument can be made that Hepworth was both paralleling scientific inquiry and exploring consciousness of a 'complex inner self' in various ways throughout her mature career, though it is not generally put this way. Her work never allows of a division between scientific and artistic or broadly humanistic epistemologies, as perhaps attested in her associations with the sculptor Gabo and the scientist Bernal. This is where its radicalism perhaps most resides, and a prime reason why it exceeds the kind of aesthetics it seems at first to demand. There is no separation in Hepworth of the human from the landscape, while there is no elision of them.

Topology, the Series and the 'Related Singular'

The philosophical shift of which the above direction and connectedness of Hepworth's work is a signifier can be elaborated in relation to the way it impacts on that ubiquitous modernist device or feature, the series. [18] The manner in which tensions are explored within the elements of Hepworth's piece constitutes an exploration of what I might call the related singular, and it is this rather than a linear or monodirectional relation that underlies the series in her work. While any series may, in a sense, be understood as predicated on an element of this related singular, the series temporality tends to the linear by definition and it is either the differences between elements in time that predominate or factors such as the way each discrete piece builds to explore some connecting thematic or formal inquiry.

In Hepworth, the series, I think, primarily relates neither to linearity, progression nor unidirectional buildup, but rather explores three-dimensional tensions of interrelation and singularity. Her series are not all of the same kind, nor do they conform to the numbered groupings that most clearly typify this mode. In the expanded sense of 'series' I am proposing, however, works with titles such as 'in echelon', 'single form', 'two forms', 'three forms' or 'sphere', 'circle' or other geometric term are *de facto* series. The same is true of other recurrent themes, and of elements within particular works.

Some idea of negative space is necessary to the series as conventionally understood. Looking at the arrangement of the forms in 'Three Forms' in this way, it is evident that there is no negative space, since the spatiality set up by the emphasis on tension between forms - comparable in some ways with her use of strings in other pieces - renders through its fluidity any straightforward notion of negative space problematic. If this is correct, the mathematical relation exemplified by these works is topological rather than geometric. At issue is boundary, verticality and the horizontal, the circular and the spaces internal and external to the work in tension with its edges. 'Three Forms', like many other pieces exploring relatedness in this way, is on a base which suggests without defining a boundary (partly because it is a practical necessity; yet no artist who has looked at Brancusi could regard a base as just a base). Singularity is provisional; plurality is always implicit, like kinetic energy.

To relate this kind of mathematical analysis to subjectivity is not a matter of sentiment. If the relation between materialism and physicalism is rethought, there are implications for understandings of abstraction. This is a difficult and intricate point, but it concerns how abstraction relates to conceptions of self, which are profoundly at issue in theorising motherhood as actuality or idea. [19] Nor is it sentimental to relate it directly to the experience of motherhood, especially of multiple birth. If 'Three Forms' concerns Rothko's 'equivalent for man's new knowledge and consciousness of his more complex inner self,' it also concerns how that inner self relates externally, taking as its starting-point the powerful female universal of parturition. But parturition takes two related singularities, so that it is also about all gendered subjectivities. It is a differentiated universal. To write of the impact of motherhood on an artist's work can be to evoke that part of the experience that is in this culture largely hidden under sentiment, which is the inescapability of the forces that forge individuals as part of other wholes. In a culture where individualism is king, and corporeal motherhood unsymbolised, such an art is not readily understood.

The other half of Rothko's articulation of the modernist split epistemology is science. Harrison appears to validate Nicholson's objectivity while preferring Rothko's exploration of the subject. The old western association between objectivity, science and masculinity persists, even though the objectivity of science has been under relentless siege for most of the last (twentieth) century. The association of both with masculinity is perhaps even harder to dislodge for reasons of cultural hegemony, despite the rise of observer-inclusive scientific methodologies.

The same association also applies to aesthetics. This is visible in the somewhat commonplace idea that objectivity can reside in consensus. If enough people think something is so, it has a certain objective truth. Though possibly unremarkable in that it underlies a broad spectrum of assumptions about aesthetics, it is actually a dangerous idea in politics. As an understanding of objectivity familiar to the adherents of prominent understandings of modernism, this hints towards the opposite end of the modernist ideological spectrum to Hepworth, its fetishised slide towards fascism. But not only. It is quite central. Greenberg suggested it in relation to aesthetic value in the sense that some works endure because there actually is some objective aesthetic value in them. This is Greenberg in the third of his Seminars on Aesthetics with a slack line of reasoning, and an initially surprising touch of realism, which I shall take up:

Certain works are singled out in their time or later as excelling, and these works continue to excel: that is they continue to compel those of us who in time after look, listen, or read hard enough. And there's no explaining this durability which creates a consensus - except by the fact that taste is ultimately objective. The best taste, that is; that taste which makes itself known by the durability of its verdicts; and in this durability lies the proof of its objectivity. [20]

This projection, which makes out of a subjective apprehension an objective existence, is actually an aspect of classic realism, and opposed to the idealised modernism with which Greenberg is associated.

In its circularity, the argument is common enough among those who believe in the objectivity of aesthetic value; it sustains large sectors of the art market. The work lasts because it has value, and its value resides in the fact that it lasts. There is a consensus that makes the work endure, and its endurance is proof of the validity of the consensus. All the old spectres are there - taste, hierarchy (the 'best' taste) hegemony, mystification ('there's no explaining this durability'), disinterestedness. It is the same fundamental myth that justifies a supposedly fixed canon.

While there may well be a place for a kind of canonical list, the justification for it is not this value-duration circularity, which merely evades the issues around historicising value, which would lead to ways of analysing the cyclical tendencies of canonical renewal. The canon is not a simple constant, though the conservative argument would have it seem so. Certain works fall into oblivion. So-called 'new classics', a dubious and recuperative term, are formed out of works that began as radical and oppositional. Certain forms are relegated to lower in the hierarchies of artistic evaluation as succeeding movements vie for ascendancy. Greenberg's slip towards realism betrays the denial involved; realism and naturalism [21] are not favoured antecedents of modernism, nor is Impressionism. They are not totally elided, but their signification is downplayed where it might challenge the dominant values. [22] In its essentials, the marginalisation of Hepworth is according to the same structural logic.

The history of Symbolism is a good example of canonical change early in the twentieth century, as is in literature T. S. Eliot's revival of the seventeenth century British Metaphysical poets, Symbolism being revived in the 1960s after a shorter term of oblivion than the Metaphysicals. Another kind of cultural amnesia comes into play, and it is easy to forget they were 'forgotten'. The detailed reasons why they had fallen out of favour and why they had returned are beyond the scope of this essay, but they should be noted when seeking to clarify the role of traditional aesthetics in the histories of the suppression and/or incorporation of all art that challenges the fixity of the canon. Its relevance to those works revisited or revived through feminisms and post-colonialists, or indeed those initially resisted and then assimilated, should be obvious, but it is masked by the mirror image of Greenberg's denial in the form of radical unease with anything that invokes aesthetic value. It is easy enough to dismiss anyone with a vested interest in change as lacking in objectivity, of course, less so those whose position coincides with the received. The subjectivity and interestedness of much aesthetic criticism since the eighteenth century is concealed, not only because of ideological dominance, but more specifically because it is appropriated to a theory of dominance.

The upheavals in art of the end of the last century were inextricable from the colonial experience and the rise of modern feminism. Most dominant accounts still have not developed analyses that fully take this on board. There is too much invested in maintaining the old paradigms; they are security in economic and psychic terms. Hepworth does not quite 'read' either in terms of dominant analysis or in terms of the necessary corrective of feminism. While there is no doubt that institutional and individual sexism are part of the reason Hepworth's contribution is difficult to assess, the prime reasons may be still more difficult to isolate. They can, however, be productively approached through reading the work.

In the histories of art, the fate of specific works and of the artists who made them is currently understood in a fairly orderly progression of styles and chronology. This progression, moreover, tends to imply a more or less explicit idea of progress. 'Primitive' forms in the hands of 'primitives' are in this account less developed than in the hands of sophisticates. I would not argue that there is no difference, nor even that there is an equivalent 'amount' of 'development' involved. But I would argue that the hierarchies with which these observations are overlaid are a serious impediment to understanding.

Much has been written about women's time as differing from that of men, and I well recall the habitual ease with which my old colonial relatives would declare that the natives had no sense of time. These differences are actual, but they are not about having no sense of time, nor are they reducible to the trivialised explanations of the rigidly superior masters. It is furthermore a differential that will be changing as a result of greater variety of experience and plurality of social structures. Significant numbers of majority world individuals move between their home land and the West. An equally noteworthy number of women move between the domestic sphere and the formal economy, and so do some men in however limited a manner. These changes are fore grounding the relativity of experiential time, but with differing starting-points which not only inflect their trace and meanings but also perhaps change them more deeply.

Women's cultural time is a strange and hybrid phenomenon. It is still different from men's. This is not only of relevance to gender-specific critique. It affects the ways women's art is read in the mainstream. This is a version of the much repeated, and much ignored, idea that the cultural production of members of any marginalised group cannot just be added in, but rather change fundamentally the histories into which they are reinserted.

This will have to suffice for the part of the point that concerns time. But it also impacts on place. The same basic difficulties arise in relation to national canons, which can be brought into play in the political arena, as has been claimed of Abstract Expressionism. The *reductio ad absurdam* would be to debate whether the Germans were lacking in objectivity to value Goethe above Shakespeare, the French, Racine, or whoever - or whether European, English or American modernism is greatest. It is a false issue arising out of the wrong question, though it persists because it is a product of competitive logic. Whatever it is that makes certain forms of art endure at certain times and in certain places requires to be rethought in non competitive, non oppositional terms, not only because of politics, but also because such terms are inimical to art. If new frameworks are being elaborated in contemporary feminist psychoanalytic criticism and aesthetics, they are not *ex nihilo*. They have their analogue in science, as can be shown, for example, in one of Einstein's ideas, though I am aware of the difficulties involved in this kind of borrowing. I introduce it partly because it is a further challenge to the objectivity-science coupling, partly because Hepworth's science is more readily comprehensible according to this later model, and partly because it is worth speculating on its rejection. It is his abandoned idea of the 'cosmological constant', and in a few moments I shall refer to it to sketch in a possible structure of a structure. This, as you may know, was the idea for which Einstein apologised. His greatest blunder, or so it seemed. He realised that the expanding universe must be countered by some other force, not opposing, but congruent. Let us suppose that, like the cosmological constant, the aesthetic is a relational constant - it maintains the same relation to a changing *socius*. I suppose it can be thought at first as a counter force, but that is something of a distortion. It may, however, suffice as a way in to rethinking relatedness. This approach can account for the generality of aesthetic forms, their variety and, crucially, their capacity to change. It is an inherently dynamic and flexible model, based not on measure and disinterest, but rather on complex interrelations. For the logic of the insistence that the aesthetic is unchanging, with durability as a prime criterion, cannot account for the art of the beginning of the twentieth century without mystification. When I say 'account for' I do not mean to suggest that art can be explained away, nor do I mean that it is reducible to argument. The aesthetic does indeed involve a move outside time and place, and therefore is not *fully* explicable with reference to them, but crucially it does not abolish time or place - it may in ways that are important to differentiate, [23] suspend, alter perceptually, reverse inside and outside, but it does not erase. It is the trace that is susceptible to analysis, somewhat like the trace of particles in physics that can only be known by their effect - or, of course, the unconscious. This fact does not diminish their explanatory power or invalidate their philosophico-material existence.

The cosmological constant is consistent with the argument about Hepworth in this chapter in two ways: it concerns elemental tensions conceived as inseparable but distinct (the series in Hepworth, for example); and it concerns universal forces in variable relation (sexed subjectivities, or female universals in tension with males that are not fixed). To adapt the phrase, the expanding *socius* is countered by that other, congruent, force, the material constant. What this implies is not a battle between oppositions, but rather a dynamic relation. It requires the reconceptualisation of the notion of expansion to incorporate contraction, ex-centricity, con-centricity, to posit a radical relationality in which the specificity of each instance does not merely count towards a generality as a kind of average or (arche)type or superior or ideal. Instead, it can determine how the greater or more general is not only *viewed* from a variety of starting points, but also *formed* by them. These are then capable of constituting a complex generality that can have genuine claims to universality without fixing one understanding as the only privileged version.

A Digression into the Void - or why is a hole in Hepworth different from a hole in Moore? [24]

Hepworth is famous for having pierced the stone. It is now quite difficult to grasp just how radical a formal move this was. It is well documented that she did it before Henry Moore, though this is not the point right now. I would argue that she did it first because going through the stone is, for her art, inevitable. It was spatially necessary. As a formal feature, the hole is important, not necessarily *qua* hole, but as a symptom of an understanding of spatiality and relatedness.

If, as I suggest, Hepworth encompasses both parts of what Rothko said, this would not be applicable to Moore; in his work, redrawing the boundaries between scientific and epistemological, objective and ontological, is not the point. (This is a comment about characterisation, not relative value; I do not say one is better than the other). Moore's work has perhaps a greater tendency towards 'the inner self', and its representation in the sense that Rothko means it, and it produces a very different idea of motherhood. (These are large generalisations, but there is, I think, enough in them for them to be at least adequately indicative.) Motherhood is indeed much more important as an explicit theme to Moore than it is to Hepworth, which is counter to gender stereotyping, as is the persistence of the scientific in her work. Ann Wagner has written fascinatingly on what this might mean for Moore [25] but at this historical moment, it seems probable that the radical woman artist, especially one of Hepworth's bent, would be drawn to rethinking 'masculine' knowledges, and there is evidence to support the argument that she did not put it this way, at least in part, for reasons of strategy. It is an element in her work that gives rise to accusations of coldness. The pursuit of clarity over tenderness or passion is rarely validated in women artists, particularly of Hepworth's generation, and her critics tend to see it as a fault (perhaps a symptom of the received incompatibility of classicism, or indeed sublime, with the feminine).

Hepworth explored motherhood as bodies in space, and holes as passages between, not absences. In her epistemology, as in Einstein's, there is no such thing as empty space. A science in which even the vacuum is not empty, and which recognises a distinction between anti-matter and non-matter, is an epistemology of connection where the point of contact is as definitional as constitutive elements.

This poses a problem for one predominant way of (re)thinking. The notion, more or less metaphorical or explicit, of 'interstices' is prevalent enough to be a significant current in radical or revisionist thought. But not so in this philosophy, of which Hepworth's work is in some senses a manifestation. [26] There are no interstices, as there are no oppositions. Interstices presuppose gaps.

Let me draw to a close by giving a resonant example, one that leads back to my starting point. Writing about Anish Kapoor, whose work bears comparison with Hepworth's in many productive ways, Homi Bhabha comments on making art out of emptiness. [27] It is a beautiful essay. Bhabha is right about the difference between an art that concerns itself with the void and one which is about the figuration of emptiness or fullness, absence or presence. But such an art is not located as he suggests in the emptiness between, in his words, those 'contrastive or contradictory states' [28], not least because though they are either contrastive or contradictory in one aspect of their relation, this is not sufficient as an account of their difference. There may be discontinuities, but they are of a different model than the interstitial one he names. The notion of the void is interesting here because it is impossible to say whether it is at bottom spatial or temporal; there is no gap. Under various guises, the currently prominent vocabulary of loopholes, gaps, spaces between and a variety of metaphors which 'make new space' in progressive cultural theory, especially feminist, may be nostalgic. It accords with a model of desire predicated on loss that may now be superseded. [29]

Gaps, then, in this account must be the sign of some form of violence or dysfunction. They will not persist, because they are unnatural in the sense that they represent a conceptual error. So if there are no breaks, gaps or empty spaces, what of transcendence? Transcendence must either be impossible, or must be amplification rather than a move elsewhere or beyond. I do not think it impossible. It is expansion and contraction at the same time. The move 'beyond' becomes an alteration of the starting point, not a departure from, abnegation or denial of, a point of origin. 'Point of origin' is both simply the starting-point and complexly the distillation - which is not to be confused with the sum - of starting-points. (This is, by the way, one reason why ethics is essential; it is also a reason why abstraction is never a simple opposition to the figurative). It contains the singular and the plural, individual and collective, in shifting, but constant relation. This is where the cosmological constant comes into its own as an analogue, because its constancy is relational: it is always the same in relation to that which is always changing.

That is what characterises the hole in Hepworth. It is how she conceives space. The late nineteenth century concerned itself much with the void - the gulf, nothingness, 'le Néant'; there was even a book called *Le Livre du Néant*, the book of the void. Hepworth and Kapoor are a very long way from that particular nothingness, which was indeed a gap, a space between, interstitial.

References and notes

1   See Christine Battersby, *The Phenomenal Woman*. Oxford, Polity, 1998, especially pp. 125-147 for an admirable investigation of this in relation to Adorno.

2   Clearly these examples are highly selective and recent. Terry Eagleton, *The Ideology of the Aesthetic*. Oxford/Cambridge Mass., Blackwell, 1990. David Carroll, *Paraesthetics*. London, Methuen, 1987. Carroll interrogates the category of the aesthetic in terms that overlap with mine, but that embrace the abolition of transcendence or the kinds of generalisation necessary for issues of gender to be approached. Frederick Jameson, on the other hand, does not deny the idea of differentiation within some kind of 'social totality', nor does he deny the connection between the individual and the universal. Though his 'political unconscious' appears as gender-blind as the thinking of the majority of Marxists outside feminism, it has within it the conceptual possibility of thinking gender. See *The Political Unconscious*. Cornell University Press 1981 and *The Geopolitical Aesthetic*. Bloomington, Indiana, 1992.

3   As is often the case when hostile commentators take on feminist concerns, Crowther's argument here is by far the weakest part of his book. It is baffling that such writers content themselves with scant research - the most recent 'gendercentric' reference in this book is 1975 - when they would not do so in relation to any other point, let alone a major philosophy.

4   There is some confusion arising out of the currency of the term 'an aesthetic'.

5   Hilde Hein and Carolyn Korsmeyer (Eds.) *Aesthetics in Feminist Perspective*. Bloomington, Indiana, 1993. Its successor has suffered the same fate; *Feminism and Tradition in Aesthetics*. See also the two very welcome Blackwell books, Korsmeyer (Ed.) *Aesthetics: The Big Questions*. Oxford/ Malden Massachusetts, Blackwell, 1998 and the brief section on aesthetics in Alison M. Jaggar and Iris Marion Young (Eds.) *A Companion to Feminist Philosophy*. Oxford/Malden Massachusetts, Blackwell, 1998.

6   Edited by Peggy Zeglin Brand and Carolyn Korsmeyer, Pennsylvania State University, 1995. See the review essay by Nicola Foster and myself in *Women's Philosophy Review*, no. 19 Autumn 1998 pp. 84-92. Also

forthcoming in 2000 are: Florence and Foster (Eds.) Special Issue on 'Aesthetics' of the *Women's Philosophy Review*, and *Differential Aesthetics* Ashgate Press. There is also a second special issue of *Hypatia* on feminist aesthetics planned, edited by Peg Brand and Mary Devereaux.

7   See notes 1 and 5 above; and Christine Battersby, *The Phenomenal Woman*. Oxford, Polity, 1998.

8   But see also Margaret Iverson, 'The Deflationary Impulse: Postmodern Feminism and the anti-aesthetic' in Andrew Benjamin and Peter Osborne (Eds.) *Thinking Art: Beyond Traditional Aesthetics*. London, ICA 1991, pp. 81-93.

9   See Battersby, *op. cit.* p.133, and Margaret Whitford, *Luce Irigaray: Philosophy in the Feminine*. London, Routledge, 1991.

10 David Thistlewood (Ed.) *Barbara Hepworth Reconsidered*. Tate Gallery/ Liverpool University Press, 1996. Charles Harrison '" Englishness" and "Modernism" Revisited', *Modernism/ Modernity*, vol. 8, no. 1, January 1999, pp. 75-90. Harrison's focus is on his own work and 'Englishness' before aesthetics; he acknowledges that the aesthetic is 'never pure or uncontingent' (p. 78), but goes on to say that in order to address modernism, what is needed is 'non-sociological ... adequately theorised in aesthetic, or formal, or, let us say, Greenbergian terms.' (p. 79) This premise, that Greenbergian formalism is adequate as a frame, is what I take issue with.

11 *Loc. cit.* pp. 23-42, 'Barbara Hepworth: the Odd Man Out? Preliminary Thoughts about a Public Artist'. The position is further developed in 'Touching Gender: the Word, the Image and the Tactile' in Martin Heusser *et al.* (Eds.) *Text and Visuality*. Amsterdam/Altlanta GA, Rodopi, 1999, pp. 271-282.

12 What is needed is something like a shift from 'enslaved-assertive' to 'spontaneous-affirmative', to borrow Lyotard's in some ways very appealing terms, which, however, make me as a woman cautious. I am not sure I want to be heard as 'spontaneous-affirmative' - perhaps informed-innovative?

13 Harrison, *loc cit.* p. 84.

14   *Ibid.* This is the exact point that I take as a misreading of a whole philosophical position in which I include my own.

15   But I would not protest the charge without reference to Deborah Knight's witty essay 'Why we enjoy condemning sentimentality: a meta-aesthetic perspective', *Journal of Aesthetics and Art Criticism*, vol. 57, no. 4, Fall 1999, pp. 411-420.

16   Hepworth was little suited to conventional ideas of sweet motherhood, and controversially put the triplets in a nursery so that she could work - with money provided by another woman, Margaret Mellis. Yet she was very far from indifferent as a mother; the pressures and contradictions are now, in some quarters at least, better understood.

17   Cited in Harrison, *op. cit.* p. 85.

18   John Klein has written on the modernist series in painting and the art market in 'The Dispersal of the Modernist Series', *Oxford Art Journal*, vol. 21, no. 1, 1998, pp. 121-135.

19   A rethinking of the material, and of however that feeds into materialism, is a fundamental. In this, as well as in relation to sex, the work of someone like Marcuse cannot serve as a model, even though he puts subjectivity at the centre and even though I agree with his spin on the Marxist insistence that art is political - that is, the premise that the political potential of art resides in art itself, in aesthetic form as such. Art is thus not necessarily specific to the interests or outlook of any particular class. Herbert Marcuse, *The Aesthetic Dimension.*(Trans. Erica Sherova) London, Macmillan, 1978.

20   My emphasis. Referenced with approval by Harrison, p. 85 and note 16.

21   *Cf.* Swinburne's distinction: 'The one is a typical example of prosaic realism, the other of poetic reality' *Studies in Shakespeare.* 1880, p. 136. Cited in *Oxford English Dictionary* under Realism. Without getting too much into the complexities, I might add that the natural religion underlying philosophical naturalism is probably the most important in what defines it from realism, in which the independent reality of the physical is prime. These do not always map onto their uses in art, literary or cultural history. The former is also a later

development than the latter.

22   The recent grip of Monet mania provoked by the Royal Academy exhibition is indicative of this in that the critical emphasis on how he prefigures Abstract Expressionism claims his work to validate the later movement rather than making a more nuanced historical argument about the radicality of Impressionism, which might raise questions about that of subsequent movements. Impressionism was associated with the feminine by critics very early in its history; abstract expressionism the opposite.

23   See below, discussion of subject-object relations in this, whether the effects are internal or external, phenomenological or noumenous.

24   Hepworth and her contemporary Henry Moore have so often been compared right from the beginning of their careers early in the twentieth century that it quickly became a cliché, rendering Hepworth less visible.

25   See "' Miss Hepworth's Stone is a Mother'" in Thistlewood, *op. cit.* pp. 53-74, esp. p. 68*ff.*

26   Irigaray would be a prime example, as her textual strategies show as clearly as her arguments. But I am not suggesting a straightforward assimilation of contemporary feminist philosophy with Einsteinian physics. The point is much more difficult to come at than this, concerning as it does catachresis, while yet acknowledging its influence.

27   Homi K. Bhabha, 'Anish Kapoor: Making Emptiness' *Anish Kapoor Exhibition Catalogue*, London 30 April - 14 June 1998, Hayward Gallery and University of California Press, p. 24 and see pp. 11- 40.

28   *Ibid.*

29   See especially Elizabeth Grosz, *Volatile Bodies: Toward a Corporeal Feminism.* Bloomington, Indiana University Press, 1994.

'A View from the Boundary':
An Aesthetic Philosopher encounters Art and its History.

Helen C. Chapman

Abstract

The relationship between aesthetics and the 'product' which it is discussing, namely artworks, has always been problematic. For while aesthetics is manifestly concerned with understanding and theorising the nature of the artwork, traditionally there has been little questioning of the art historical processes which lie behind the objects thus sustaining the relationship between canonic art history and aesthetic theory. While recent art history has been forced to question the tenets upon which its methodologies are based, philosophical aesthetics has often failed to recognise these changes. I shall argue that this leads to a situation where there is a fundamental mismatch between contemporary art practice and the different histories which are being exposed and the theoretical tools which are available for the aesthetician, thus reinforcing the theory practice hierarchical divide. In this situation, it is not the theory which is questioned, but rather the adequacy of the work itself. Theory judges the work to not fit its paradigms therefore it is not effective. This paper will address how this situation can be challenged thus enabling the emergence of a more responsive aesthetic discourse

In 1993 the *Journal of Aesthetics and Art Criticism* marked its fiftieth year of existence by commissioning a commemorative issue. As Lydia Goehr writes in her opening editorial, the intention of this issue was to celebrate the achievements of the journal and the American Society for Aesthetics. The articles it contains are intended to 'mark both an ending and a beginning' [1]; i.e., they look back over some of the debates of the previous fifty years and look forward to how the discipline can develop in the future. In responding to this request for reflection several contributors chose to interrogate John Passmore's well known and somewhat notorious article published initially in 1950 entitled 'The Dreariness of Aesthetics'. [2] In these articles the authors attempt to vindicate aesthetics from Passmore's attack and to show its continuing relevance to contemporary debate. However, in reading through these articles I was struck by how, in the main, they fail to challenge Passmore's diagnosis. The articles - with one or two notable exceptions - *are* dull. What links them in their dullness is their singular failure to address art practice and history directly, if in some cases at all. Even when art-works are addressed the choice of 'example' is more often than not hackneyed and canonical. In fact, a reader who approaches the journal unaware of the 'subject' matter or 'content' of aesthetic debate could easily come away with an understanding of the discipline that contained little reference to art objects at all. The debate that occurs within the pages of the journal is hermetic: it speaks *of* and *to* a tradition which has developed a theoretical determination of its purpose, one which is increasingly divorced from the subject matter it is putatively about.

My response to reading this journal has resonances with my experience of teaching aesthetics to undergraduate and graduate students from a variety of backgrounds. While students are keen to explore questions such as 'What makes an object a work of art?' and/or 'Why do we value some works of art more than others?', they are often singularly unimpressed with the theories and explanations which philosophy offers. They quickly and intuitively grasp that there is a disjunction between the claims that the theory is making and the 'examples' they are examining. Aesthetic phenomena - be it art or literature - can be *made* to fit a particular theory, but students will question the validity of 'imposing' a theoretical reading which fails to fully elucidate the object. Furthermore, they often question the veracity and 'use' of theories which on analysis appear to address a very limited understanding of aesthetic practice.

In examining these two examples it could be argued that my students and I are simply failing to grasp the function of philosophical aesthetics. Aesthetics is not intended to directly address the work of art. It is a theoretical discourse which by its definition *is* and *must be* abstract. To focus directly on specific artworks is to engage in art criticism and/or art history not philosophy. I am simply misguided to expect to find an aesthetic discourse which addresses concerns within contemporary practice.

In response to this I would argue that while in part this argument is true - a traditional understanding of philosophical aesthetics does conceive its task in terms of metacriticism and abstraction - it does not mean that a philosophical approach to the artwork must always be conducted in this way. It is not necessary to be limited to a view of aesthetics which is self-referential and often 'dull'. I want to argue that on the contrary, philosophical aesthetics can be a more interesting and relevant pursuit, but to be so it must question and challenge some of the preconceptions which it holds. In particular, it must look afresh at its relationship to its cognate disciplines and the 'practice' which it is discussing.

One of the reasons why philosophical aesthetics has tended towards the 'dreary' is that it has often failed to incorporate the form of questioning which these other disciplines have undergone. It has not challenged the starting points from which its analysis is developed, but retreats behind the boundaries of the 'accepted' disciplinary discourse rather than questioning the boundaries themselves. As I shall show, even when alternative voices are raised within the discipline, their potential radicality is often diminished by a failure to question a deep rooted identity as a *philosopher* of aesthetics and the assumptions which this appellation entails. This means that despite protestations to the contrary, the artwork is still viewed as *subsidiary* to philosophy. Thus my intention here is to examine how it may be possible to develop a more reciprocal relationship between aesthetic theory and the art object. In so doing I shall argue that only then might a position be developed to enable a more responsive and responsible understanding of both the artwork and theory.

In the first section of this paper I shall demonstrate how, even when philosophical aestheticians are apparently challenging the boundaries of the discipline, they have a tendency to retreat back to entrenched and problematic positions. Then in the light of this discussion and the problems it exposes, I shall start to suggest how it may be possible to develop an aesthetic approach which is sensitive to the problematic relationship between theory and practice.

Part one

In selecting a 'figure' to exemplify the problems of contemporary analytical aesthetics it would be easy to have alighted on one who is seen to be very much part of the established tradition. [3] However, instead, I want to explore aspects of the arguments which Arthur Danto has developed over the last twenty years in texts such as *Transfiguration of the Commonplace*, and *The Philosophical Disenfranchisement of Art*. Danto is an interesting figure to use because on first reading it appears that he contradicts the position which I set up in the introduction. He is a philosopher who *does* discuss contemporary art practice and art history, and his view of aesthetic discourse is not ahistorical. Furthermore as I shall argue, aspects of his analysis can usefully be used to show why philosophical aesthetics could and should be able to challenge the preconceptions which sustain it. However, as I shall demonstrate, Danto's work also exemplifies a certain more problematic view concerning the relationship between aesthetic theory and cognate disciplines. Danto's 'Jekyll and Hyde' philosophical persona can therefore be used both to address the question as to how and why philosophical aesthetics can be questioned, while simultaneously demonstrating why it is necessary to move beyond the position which he advocates.

In the space available here it is not possible - nor probably necessary - to offer an all embracing and detailed account of Danto's work. Instead I shall highlight three key aspects which can be used to exemplify the tensions which it contains. These are:

• the definition of the aesthetic object by 'The Artworld',

• the understanding of the relationship between philosophy and art history/ theory which the adoption of the concept of the 'artworld' facilitates, and

• the role of art and philosophy after the 'end of art' has been declared.

Danto first came to prominence in the 1960's with his article 'The Artworld'. [4] In this text Danto argues that any attempt to give an abstract account of what makes an object a work of art is fundamentally flawed. Even those accounts which appear on the surface to be entirely divorced from art history and practice, are informed by the cultural assumption that there is such a thing as an art object. No object has an *a priori* existence as an aesthetic object. Rather, aesthetic objects come about by virtue of the fact that they can be referred back to 'theories of the Artworld' which, as the title of Danto's book *Transfiguration of the Commonplace* suggests, transforms objects into artworks. He writes:

To see something as art at all demands nothing less than this, an atmosphere of artistic theory, a knowledge of the history of art. Art is the kind of thing that depends for its existence upon theories; without theories of art, black paint is just paint and nothing more. [5]

On first reading it may appear strange that I am suggesting that Danto's work can be used to begin to question and challenge the idea that aesthetic theory is necessarily distanced from the art object. For in the above remarks it initially seems as though he comes down entirely on the side of theory; so much so that he is advocating the impossibility of a 'non'-theoretical understanding of the art object. However, it is necessary to understand how Danto is using the term 'theory' in this instance. As stated earlier, he is attacking those critics who have argued that an aesthetic object contains an intrinsic aesthetic quality within itself. However, the paradigm case that proves the exception to this argument is to be found with objects such as Duchamp's ready-mades or, for Danto, Warhol's Brillo Boxes. For the theorist who holds to an aesthetic 'essentialist' position these objects are a problem for they contradict the idea that an aesthetic object is always intrinsically just that. In Danto's opinion essentialist theories are shown to be fundamentally flawed in that they cannot account for many aspects of twentieth century art practice. This is why he suggests that what makes an object a work of art is the way in which it can be located within a theory of art. This theory shows how art emerges as a result of a series of historical and theoretical discourses which describe objects in terms of aesthetic criteria. As Danto remarks art theory is then 'so powerful a thing as to detach objects from the real world and make them part of a different world, an art world, a world of interpreted things.' [6]

This definition of the function of the artworld is important because it allows Danto to account for how objects such as Warhol's Brillo Boxes become works of art. They can be placed within a set of critical practices and theories which bestow on them the 'status' of art object. It is because the objects have been interpreted by the artworld as *art* objects that they are able to be transformed. Furthermore, as Danto argues, the relationship between objects in the artworld is not arbitrary. There is an 'evolutionary' aspect to the process of interpretation that occurs. No artist or writer creates in a vacuum; they are products of their culture and the 'interpretative' milieu that surrounds them. Even the avant-garde's claim to make the radical break with tradition contains within itself an implicit recognition of that which it is rebelling against. Hence there is a need for aesthetics to *not* distance itself entirely from art history or theory, because this history both informs and delineates the aesthetic object. The idea of the 'artworld' which Danto is proposing is not an ahistorical or abstract concept, rather, it emerges out of and highlights the cultural and historical imperatives which surround the aesthetic object.

The value of Danto's theory is that it forces aesthetics to engage with cognate disciplines in order to explore and explain the phenomena it is analysing. Aesthetic theory is *itself* a product of the artworld; it emerges out of the continuing symbiotic relationship between practice and theory. This means that aesthetic theory by definition cannot be seen as purely abstract, nor can it be viewed entirely as the 'master discourse' which offers explanations or judgements on the phenomena which is brought before its eyes. Aesthetics is transformed by the objects which it encounters as potential candidates for inclusion in the 'artworld'. A dialectical relationship is continually in play between object and theory, however much the theory may argue to the contrary. It is this realisation of the dialectical relationship between the art object and theory that leads to the second of the aspects of Danto's theory which I want to highlight. As I argued in the introduction, philosophical aesthetics often seems to be a hermetic pursuit. The questions which are raised mean that the artwork is discussed in an abstract and distanced way, but Danto's work can show how this appearance of distance is not legitimate.

For example, while on the surface it may appear that Bell and Fry's theory of 'significant form' is a revised statement of aspects of Kant's work, it can equally be read as a theory which responds to modernist painting, in particular cubism, and in so doing legitimates its claim to be art. [7] Thus, philosophical aesthetics' claim to neutrality and universality can also be called into question. In fact as Danto argues in his text *The Philosophical Disenfranchisement of Art*, the historical account of the different philosophical interpretations of the aesthetic object can be interpreted as an attempt by philosophy to control and neutralise its potentially disruptive aspects. In Danto's view philosophy has developed theoretical explanations of the nature of the artwork which

alternate between the analytical effort to ephemeralize and hence defuse art, or to allow a degree of validity to art by treating it as doing what philosophy itself does, only uncouthly. [8]

This claim can be used to help to explain the inherently conservative aspect of philosophical aesthetics. Aesthetic objects challenge some of the tenets which traditional philosophy holds dear. For example, as Plato so definitively shows, the artist is a threat because their practice blurs the distinction between the real and the illusory. Furthermore, if a philosophical system is premised upon the validity of this distinction then it cannot allow such challenges to persist. Hence the expulsion of the poets from the Republic and the attempts which Plato makes to denigrate the products of their labours. [9] Philosophy wants and needs to protect itself against the challenges which the aesthetic raises. Therefore it is unsurprising if the space it designates to the artwork is seen as secondary to mainstream philosophical thought *and* the ideas which it develops and sustains are always in the service of repression. In Danto's opinion the 'history of philosophy itself might almost be regarded as massive collaboration to neutralize an activity'. [10]

I consider that these two aspects of Danto's theory are valuable in that they provide an analysis which exposes some of the implicit assumptions philosophy itself has employed in *its* analysis of the aesthetic object. It shows how the aesthetic object has been elevated and/or denigrated within philosophy in order to quell the questions it raises for these systems. It also shows why it is possible to question some of the apparently sacrosanct assumptions which aesthetic theory employs, such as the claim that aesthetic judgements must be 'disinterested'. By determining its field of study in this way aesthetics has prevented discussions being raised which may challenge this viewpoint. This is because questions concerning the historical, political or economic aspects of art can be automatically judged as not part of aesthetic debate and therefore ruled to be illegitimate. However, what Danto's analysis demonstrates is that these questions are implicitly present within the assumptions that philosophy has used to set up its claim about the object. Pure aesthetic judgements can be pure and disinterested, precisely because they have already decided in advance - albeit consciously or unconsciously - in what purity consists. [11]

After exposing the mechanisms through which philosophy has controlled the aesthetic object, Danto then moves to making his most radical and as I shall show, problematic claim about the artwork. He argues that work such as Warhol's 'Brillo Boxes' should be understood as marking the 'end of art.' What Danto means by this rather imperious phrase is that art has 'ended' insofar as the philosophical over-determinism of the aesthetic object is now being challenged, i.e., that 'art' as it has hitherto been defined is coming to an end. Art can free itself from the shackles of philosophy and move forward on its own terms. Danto finds the evidence to support this claim in the aesthetic practice of the twentieth century which highlights the redundancy of philosophical aesthetics *precisely because it embodies philosophical questioning*. The artwork no longer needs the philosopher to 'explain' what it is and how it should be interpreted. Instead, it takes on this task by itself. For example, in making the claim for its status as an aesthetic object Duchamp's 'Urinal' embodies and displays the philosophical question of 'why is this object art while an identical object is not?' As Danto remarks, 'art ends with the advent of its own philosophy'. [12] Therefore, if artworks are capable of 'asking' philosophical questions the role of philosophy is fundamentally called into question.

Or so one would have thought. However, it is just when the naïve reader would expect Danto to start arguing for an approach to philosophical aesthetics which would respect and respond to the state of plurality which identifies contemporary aesthetic practice that the opposite occurs. His argument, instead of trying to establish a dialogue between practice and theory whereby each mutually informs, interacts with and embellishes the other, retreats back behind the walls of abstraction. At the end of an essay on the plurality of contemporary aesthetic practice he concludes that while plurality is to be celebrated and supported because it shows that the 'end of art' has occurred, this does not mean that the role of philosophical aesthetics becomes redundant. In fact Danto suggests an even more abstract conception of aesthetics and writes:

In my view a philosophy of art worthy of the name must be worked out at a level of abstractness so general that you cannot deduce from it the form of any specific style of art. It should have application to modern and ancient art, to Eastern and Western art, to representational and to abstract art. Since everything which is art has to conform to theory if it is any good at all, no art better exemplifies it than any other. So if it is a good theory, history cannot overthrow it, and if history can, then it is not philosophy but criticism. [13]

Despite advocating and supporting the eclecticism of contemporary aesthetic practice, Danto still insists that a contemporary *philosophy* of art must be universal and abstract. How can this position be sustained, particularly in the light of the arguments he developed, and which I have outlined here, concerning the relationship of art history and philosophy?

An answer to these questions can be found by examining the underlying philosophical presumptions which have motivated Danto's work. Danto's arguments concerning the need to historicise the aesthetic object and his attack on the philosophical over-determinations of the aesthetic object occur because of his commitment to a Hegelian view of the nature of the progress of thought. Hegel's philosophy advocates a view of the history of thought as the continual dialectical progression of spirit towards self-knowledge. In the *Phenomenology of Spirit*, one of the stages which spirit manifests itself is through the aesthetic object. In its engagement with the aesthetic, spirit is able to further progress in and through its path to self-awareness and knowledge. [14] Therefore, Danto's concern with understanding aesthetic phenomena from a historical and contextual perspective is driven by his prior commitment to the Hegelian view of history understood as the dialectical progression of Spirit. This means that in a certain sense, the theory which Danto has developed has to be understood as falling prey to the theoretical over determination which he has accused past aesthetic theorists of displaying. While I have argued that Danto's reference to history and practice is to be welcomed, it must also be subject to scrutiny and question, because the methodology which underpins Danto's view of the historical progression and development of art history is determined by the Hegelian schema from which it derives. This point can be substantiated by closer analysis of the view of art history which he puts forward which is evolutionary and progressive. The narrative explains the development of art practice in terms of a gradual move from purely representative painting towards the emergence of an avant-garde. It is in this avant-garde that

the artwork is so irradiated by theoretical consciousness that the division between object and subject is all but overcome and it little matters whether art is philosophy in action or philosophy is art in thought. [15]

Underpinning both ends of this narrative is a belief in aesthetic objects as mimetic objects; i.e., they are themselves capable of 'representing' the world or the ideas they embody. Therefore the 'examples' which he uses to illustrate both the narrative of the history of art *and* the development of philosophical aesthetics are chosen because they fit the theoretical 'story' which he is telling. This theoretical story is concerned with demonstrating that art is capable of representing 'ideas' and that by engaging with the aesthetic object we are able to gain access to these ideas. Conversely, the philosophical narrative that Danto subscribes to is one which acts, as I have shown, to neutralize these 'ideas' and to downplay the role of the aesthetic. When other theories of art are discussed - for example, the expressive theory - they are not viewed on their own terms, rather they are explained and subsumed under the 'grand narrative' with which he is operating. [16]

The overall effect of the metacritical assumptions which Danto is working with is to prevent an alternative reading or history being given. There is no place for discussion of the history of art in terms of disjunction and disruption. The individual histories of art practice and theoretical discourses and also the relationships between them is understood in terms of continual transmission and progress. This partly helps to explain why in discussing the history of art, Danto's main choice of historical narrators are conservative figures such as Gombrich. His 'story' is one which cannot allow the history of art to contain gaps or fissures. Thus, figures who may challenge the narrative of representation which he is developing are ignored or distorted. Even the avant-garde is brought into the fold by reading the work in terms of the consummation of the story. Therefore it should not be surprising at this juncture to find that 'after the end of art' Danto retreats back to advocating a purely 'philosophical' understanding of the nature of artwork. Despite appearances to the contrary, I would argue that Danto uses the history of art within his discussion not because he considers that the contextualisation of aesthetic discourse is necessary to enable it to speak *of* and *to* the artwork, but because his prior philosophical beliefs tell him it should be so.

Danto's aesthetics, therefore, remains metacritical. Moreover, it contains an implicit value judgement regarding the relationship between theory and practice, philosophy and art. Art needs philosophy not as a companion in dialogue, but rather in order to explain what it does. Philosophy and the philosophers are still held to be the dominant partners. While Danto exposes and implicitly criticises previous aesthetic theories for the way in which they denigrate or marginalise the aesthetic object, he replays the same process within his own work. Despite his apparent arguments to the contrary he is still adhering to a very traditional view of the relation between disciplines. This is not only disappointing, but also does little to alleviate the situation which I described in the Introduction whereby aesthetic philosophy is viewed as a moribund and sterile discipline. However, for change to occur it is necessary for philosophy - and perhaps more pertinently philosophers - to question some of the presumptions it maintains when it comes into dialogue with the art work.

Part two - Reawakening aesthetics

I began this discussion with reference to the fiftieth anniversary edition of the *Journal of Aesthetics and Art Criticism*, asserting that many of the articles reflect the 'dullness' of aesthetics. However, this assessment was perhaps a little too acerbic and premature. While on the surface the journal appears to want to maintain a veneer of disciplinary 'respectability' and 'integrity' there is also an interesting subtext running through much of the discussion which is concerned with the relationship between the articles within the journal and the 'artworld' itself. Several of the contributors argue that in order for such a journal to develop and be of value in the next fifty years it must be willing to engage more directly with practitioners and academics working with other disciplines. This viewpoint is exemplified by the title of Anita Silvers' interesting article 'Aesthetics for art's sake, not for philosophy's!' [17] Hers is a challenging sentiment which reverses the traditional hierarchical relationship between aesthetic discourse and practice. Other contributors to the journal are more cautious about what such a suggestion may entail. However, as I shall now argue, this caution while understandable, can and should be questioned.

The reservations which the contributors express - be it implicitly or explicitly - take three different but interrelated forms. First there is a sense that in engaging with practice and art history aestheticians are wandering away from their home territory. They do not necessarily have the necessary skills or knowledges to make telling readings and judgements. But in response to such a warning I would argue that while unease may be experienced initially, it should not prevent dialogue and learning occurring. By identifying the position from which one is speaking - much as I hope I have done in this chapter - it is possible to engage and learn from the practitioners of cognate disciplines. Perhaps what is most disturbing about this approach is the fact that one is initially disarmed when entering into discussion with a 'foreign' territory. The 'armour' and back-up weapons systems normally supplied by one's disciplinary specialism are not in place. However, this is not necessarily a bad position to be in. Too often within academic debate refuge is complacently and lazily sought behind acquired knowledge which in turn becomes a retreat from listening to what the interlocutor has to say. But, by placing oneself in the position of 'student' in relationship to others, it is possible to gain a broader perspective as well as insights which can be used not only to transform the margins of areas of interest, but to impinge on 'mainstream' work as well. Anxiety about disciplinary integrity is itself a barrier to dialogue. If one can start to move away from the idea that it is continually necessary to prove and maintain a 'specialist' competency at all costs then I would argue that a position might be reached in which it is possible to move toward freer debate and thought.

The second reservation that some of the journal's contributors have is that they will lose their identity as 'aesthetic philosophers' if they challenge the traditional separation of aesthetics and art criticism/practice. Built in to this debate is a set of questions about the nature of philosophy itself. For example, if one talks about aspects of aesthetic debate via an analysis of a specific aesthetic object, is this 'aesthetics' or simply 'art' criticism?

As I argued in relation to Danto's work, the history of aesthetic philosophy has privileged terms such as abstraction, universality and disinterest. This means that philosophy has an inbuilt mechanism of critique which it can use against anyone who attempts to think about how the discipline might develop differently. However, there are no a priori reasons why an approach that engages in dialogue with the artwork 'is not philosophical'. Indeed, I hope I have shown in my discussion of Danto that it is precisely when a thinker approaches the aesthetic with too strict a philosophical framework that they can become blinded to alternative approaches and interpretations. In fact other 'aesthetic' philosophers have argued that it is necessary to try to engage in philosophical aesthetics via a dialogue with the artwork precisely because they have become aware of the problems that abstraction has raised. As Andrew Benjamin and Peter Osborne write in their editors' introduction to a collection of papers given at the Institute of Contemporary Arts in the early 1990's:

Philosophy, which had sought to remain above the critical interpretation of individual works ... is compelled to descend to their level to clarify and assess the claims about art that they embody. [18]

There needs to be a meeting point and dialogue between the disciplines which takes as its starting point the assumptions which each hold about the other. For example, one presupposition that may fruitfully be explored is to be found within the above statement, namely the age-old hierarchical ordering of theory above practice.

Finally, there is a further reservation which holds back dialogue concerns the type of 'philosophising' that an engagement with the aesthetic object will generate. In discussing individual works there is the possibility - or more accurately, inevitability - that the 'aesthetician' will be exposed not simply as a 'disembodied' set of ideas, but rather as a thinker who emerges out of particular historical, cultural context. Thus the judgements and theories which are proposed will not be universal or neutral. This again challenges how traditional philosophy conceives of its task, exposing its proponent to the charge that they are no longer a 'philosopher', but a 'cultural' critic. However, again I would argue that this accusation is ill founded. Much work within contemporary epistemology has challenged the 'myth' of the omnipotent observer who is able to make value neutral, impartial judgements. Therefore, by transposing aspects of this epistemology into the way one approaches aesthetic debate, it is possible to find 'philosophical' justification and grounding for what on the surface could seem to be simply 'subjective' opinion. [19]

I want, therefore to re-affirm the argument that while anxieties do exist in suggesting that it is necessary to approach aesthetic debate differently, the problems are not insurmountable. This is a risk which could - and should - be worth taking for both theorists and practitioners. If we are serious about moving debate and dialogue forward it is necessary for us to rid ourselves of the 'disciplinary' prejudices which we hold. Only when prejudices are challenged will it be possible to engage in dialogue which is both responsive and responsible. This will have implications not only for an individual's own work but also for how the teaching and dissemination of specific disciplines is approached. In arguing for a 'responsive' dialogue I am not suggesting that the past should be entirely forgotten; such utopian points of view are both impracticable and impossible. Instead, what I am suggesting is that by establishing a dialogue with artists, art and art history, the old questions are returned to anew.

To conclude I will briefly suggest one form this dialogue could possibly take. In his essay 'On Painting and Presence' Jean Luc Nancy engages in a dialogue with the work of the French painter François Martin. His theme - ostensibly - is the age old question 'in what way can art be said to represent the world?' However, this question is not raised by merely constructing a 'theoretical' discourse 'about' Martin's work. Instead, by using a variety of stylistical devices, he talks with and to the practitioner and his work. What I find particularly intriguing about the essay is the way in which it continually draws attention to the inadequacy of Nancy's own discourse to address the precise question he wants to ask of the painting. This is not a logical argument about how the painting 'manifests' or 'demonstrates' the issues of presence and representation suggested by the title, but a hesitancy and an acknowledgement of the problems that the writer is experiencing. Even when the most definitive statement is made about an aspect of Martin's work, it is undercut and questioned by another authorial voice. The reader is confronted with a text that itself attempts to enact the 'experience' of engaging in a dialogue with the aesthetic object. No 'theory' of presence or representation emerges at the end of the text. After finishing the text the reader might experientially 'know' more about the issues that the question of representation raises, but is left to question and draw his or her own responses to the problems that have been detailed. The open ended nature of the dialogue is important because it mirrors the encounter with the artwork.

I can imagine that the traditional aesthetician - perhaps some of the readers and participants in the *Journal of Aesthetics and Art Criticism* - would find Nancy's article neither intelligible nor a demonstration of good 'aesthetic' discourse. In fact this possibility is directly addressed by an exchange between two of the 'voices' found in the text. These remarks encapsulate not only the problems which I have outlined throughout this paper, but also the attitude and response that can be adopted in the attempt to 'think differently' about the boundaries between disciplines.

The traditionalist - exasperated at the questions and style which the main voice uses, cuts off the debate:

That does it - your clowning is tiresome

to which the other interlocutor replies,

I'm sure it is. But your obstinence [sic] *in taking painting as an object, an object of knowledge and an object of taste is no less tiresome to me. You manipulate it with delicate instruments, you make a profession of respecting its silence, but what a bore ...Why don't you rub against a little wet paint; actually your suit could use some colour.* [20]

This is the challenge we need to confront - to be prepared as theorists and academics to 'rub up' against other disciplines rather than remaining aloof and 'terribly clean'. We must be prepared 'to get ourselves mucky'. In so doing we are taking the first steps toward being participants in a dialogue with the work and the practitioner. Too often, aesthetics has taken the form of a monologue whereby the philosopher tells the practitioner what he or she is doing and what their work 'means'. It is a one-sided speech which dictates a point of view from a position of theoretical authority. As we have seen it is therefore not surprising that such work is considered to be increasingly irrelevant. Its irrelevancy derives partly from the failure to establish responsive and responsible dialogue. What Jean Luc Nancy's essay clearly demonstrates is that when true dialogue starts to develop it is beneficial for *both* participants. The practitioner can feel that their own concerns and questions are being addressed and that their voice is being heard as an equal. Furthermore, it also enables the assumptions which the aesthetician holds to be exposed and questioned. In Nancy's article this is demonstrated by the way in which 'traditional' themes such as the relationship between painting and representation are re-opened and considered anew. The dialogue with the aesthetic object and practitioner enables the philosopher to re-assess their own understanding of questions which perhaps all too often they have presupposed to be answered and closed.

It is the possibility for re-assessment on both sides which this 'mucky' approach offers that I find worth considering. The risk-taking that this dialogue involves is valuable precisely because it offers the possibility that I as a philosopher will have my own assumptions and presuppositions questioned and challenged. I can develop *as* a philosopher in a dialogue with the practitioner and the aesthetic object which they produce. Surely the possibilities of renewal and challenge which this approach facilitates means that the earlier cautions and reservations should and must be put aside. And one never knows, by adopting this approach it may perhaps even be possible to suggest that aesthetics may start to become 'less dreary'. I, for one, certainly hope this is the case. So, then, who wants to talk ...?

References and notes

1   Goehr, Lydia. Editorial *Journal of Aesthetics and Art Criticism*, Vol 51.2, Spring 1993, p. *v.*

2   Passmore, John. 'The Dreariness of Aesthetics' *Mind*, Vol 60, 1951.

3   Here I have in mind figures from analytical aesthetics such as Bullough or Sibley. However, in many ways these would be a too easy target for the argument I am developing here, insofar as the project with which they are concerned makes no attempt to see aesthetics as a discipline which engages with the artwork. They come from a philosophical tradition which defines aesthetics in terms of abstraction and logical analysis.

4   Danto, Arthur. 'The Artworld' *The Journal of Philosophy*, 61, no. 19, 1964, pp. 571-584.

5   Danto, Arthur. *Transfiguration of the Commonplace*. Harvard University Press, 1981, p. 135.

6   *Ibid*.

7   See Clive Bell's influential text *Art*. London and New York Chatto and Windus, 1958, which was originally published in 1914. Here Bell argues that what distinguishes an aesthetic object from everyday objects is whether it possesses what is termed 'significant form'. This is what attracts and captivates the viewer. Art is not concerned with representation; it does not matter what a work depicts, rather what is of interest is its internal form. This theory is often read as a 20th century reworking of Kant's argument that aesthetic pleasure is a 'disinterested' pleasure, rather than it being seen as a defence of cubism.

8   Danto, Arthur. *The Philosophical Disenfranchisement of Art*. Columbia University Press, 1986, p. 7.

9   See Plato, *Republic*. (Trans. A. Bloom) Basic Books Inc. 1968. Plato's arguments against artists and art can be found in Book 10 of the Republic. Interestingly, although Plato expels the poets and artists from the Republic he

also implicitly honours and recognises their - disruptive - skills. The ceremony described in the *Republic* which is used to expel them from the city has been identified as the rites of scapegoating and ostracism whereby a person is chosen as sacrificial victim, is honoured by the city for a year and then is cast out from within its confines. (For discussion of this ritual and its place in Plato's text see J. P. Vernant. *Myth and Tragedy in Ancient Greece*. Zone Books, 1990, pp. 132 - 5).

10   Danto. 1986, *op cit*. p. 4.

11   A similar argument can be found in the work of Pierre Bourdieu. In his article 'The Historical Genesis of a Pure Aesthetic'. *The Journal of Aesthetics and Art Criticism*. 1987, Vol No XLVI pp. 201-211, Bourdieu writes 'the pure thinker, by taking as the subject of his own reflection his own experience - the experience of a cultured person from a certain social milieu - but without focusing on the historicity of the object to which it is applied (and by considering it a pure experience of the work of art) unwittingly establishes this singular experience as a transhistorical norm for every aesthetic perception. Now this experience, with all the aspects of singularity that it appears to possess (and the feeling of uniqueness probably contributes greatly to its worth) is itself an institution which is the product of historical intervention and whose *raison d'être* can be reassessed only through an analysis which is itself purely historical'. p. 202.

12   Danto, 1986 *op cit*. p. 107.

13   Danto, Arthur 'Learning to Live with Pluralism' in *The Wake of Art: Criticism, Philosophy and the End of Taste*. G. Horowitz and T. Huhn (Eds.) G + B Arts International, 1998, p. 94.

14   Hegel, G. W. F. *Phenomenology of Spirit*. (Transl. A. V. Miller) Oxford University Press, 1977, Section VII part B. Also, as Michael Inwood points out in the entry on aesthetics in *A Hegel Dictionary*. Blackwell, 1992 Hegel also develops these arguments in the *Encyclopaedia* where in section III 'art forms together with religion and philosophy, a part of Absolute Spirit ... Art ... has a rational, cognitive value: it progressively reveals the nature of the world, or man and the relationship between them (the absolute) in a sensuous form or the form of intuition [Anschauung].' p. 42.

15   Danto. 1987, *op cit*. p. 113.

16   See Danto. 1986, *op. cit*. pp. 108-110. Here Danto performs a sleight of hand whereby what he identifies as the failure of theories such as the 'Expression Theory of Art' are viewed as symptomatic of the move toward the 'end of art'. Aesthetics no longer needs individual theories to answer the question 'what is art', rather it needs Hegel's meta-theory which explains the 'narrative' of the failure of the other aesthetic theories.

17   Silvers, Anita. *Journal of Aesthetics and Art Criticism*, 1993, *op. cit*. pp. 141-150. These themes are mirrored by Gordon Epperson's remarks in the 'reminiscences' section of the volume where he comments: 'I have often wondered why aestheticians are reluctant to 'compare notes' as it were, with living composers and performing artists. There seems to have been in the early days of the Journal, greater openness to a kind of cross-fertilisation - entertained, at any rate, as a possibility - between aestheticians and artists; and its tone was less exclusively academic. I would like to see a similar openness today, without the sacrifice of philosophical rigour.' p. 284.

18   Benjamin, A. & Osborne, P. *Thinking Art: Beyond Traditional Aesthetics*. ICA Publications, 1991, p. XI.

19   For example, recent work in feminist epistemology has stressed the idea of situated knowledges and the 'standpoint' of each particular claim. See for example the work of Donna Haraway in *Simians, Cyborgs and Women*. Free Association Books, 1991 and Sandra Harding, *Whose Science, Whose Knowledge?* Open University, 1991. I would argue that productive links could start to be made between the methodologies which these theories are advocating and innovative approaches to aesthetic enquiry.

20   Nancy, Jean-Luc, 'On Painting (and) Presence' in *The Birth to Presence*. (Trans. B. Holmes) Stanford University Press, 1993, p. 351.

Frameworks of Theory and Practice:
Looking at class, 'race' and gender in visual culture history.

Gen Doy

Abstract

In the ways I teach art history, drawing on ongoing work primarily with MA students, a key aim is to encourage students to relate theory and practice. While apparently an obvious thing to do, this is deceptively difficult, and depends on what theories and what practices we are talking about. I will explain how I see a Marxist 'framework' or theoretical basis as helpful and enabling rather than 'economistic' or reductive', as critics of Marxism would have it. Within this overarching framework, I try to understand the interplay of issues concerning class, 'race' and gender in visual culture, theory and practice. The relative weight of these issues shifts according to various contextual factors as well as which examples of art works we are studying. One of the best indicators of the success of theories and teaching strategies is when the students can go away and 'do it themselves' without a tutor. Maybe what I'm aiming for is something like Walter Benjamin's 'Author as Producer', i.e. 'art historian as producer'! I hope so.

In this chapter, I want to discuss the relationship of theory and practice in the teaching of visual culture history. While apparently a very obvious thing to do, this is not as easy as it sounds, either for the teacher or the students. A few years ago an external examiner whose main area of expertise was desktop publishing, criticised the section on 'aims and objectives' in one of my course booklets. In this section, I stated that my main aim was to encourage and enable students to apply their knowledge of theoretical texts to the analysis of examples of visual culture, and I added that any student who did this successfully would pass the course. The said examiner informed me that this was not demanding enough, and further, that my course was 'too modernist' and 'not postmodern enough'. At first I assumed that these comments were made because the course dealt with the theories of Marx and Freud, among others, two of the old white bearded men of modernism. However much later, I began to wonder whether this examiner's dislike of my course and its basis had something to do with my ideas about theory and practice. [1] For example, I assumed that theory was enabling for students, and allowed them to progress to a greater understanding of culture, and also that theories do not exist for their own sakes but should be tested out in practice. These supposedly 'modernist' notions of theory are often looked on now as crude and unnuanced.

In addition, any approach which involves Marxism is looked on as economistic, reductive and simply no longer of any relevance. In favour are

1   notions of theory as not necessarily related to the world but as a discrete discourse;

2   the irrelevance of the real or reality as objects of theorising; and

3   the invention of new concepts which purport to designate developments or situations never before seen in history which require a new kind of critical language to refer to them.

Take as an example of this some of the writings of Homi K. Bhabha, and his notions of hybridity, mimicry and in-betweenness. [2] Students have so much trouble deciphering what some postmodern and post colonial critics mean, that they think their task is done when they put the book down after struggling for hours to understand it. What is then necessary, though, is for students to position themselves in relation to these theoretical writings, and assess their usefulness. One of the problems with postmodern writers' rejection of so-called master-narratives and totalising theories is that it can be experienced as enabling and empowering for some lecturers and students, caught up in an exciting kaleidoscope of shifting, decentred identities, positionalities and ethnicities, yet, for many, these theories which argue against agency, experience, history and in some extreme cases even reality, can be profoundly confusing and disorienting. This is not necessarily beneficial, nor does it result often in an ideological opposition to the status quo. And it is not only postmodern theorists who reject totalising theories. Linda Nochlin wrote in the introduction to her recent book, *Representing Women*, that she rejects the idea of a single theoretical or methodological approach to the study of art history. At first sight this seems odd, given that for many years Nochlin's approach to art history would have definitely been described as feminist. She questions

the possibility of a single methodology - empirical, theoretical, or both, or neither - which is guaranteed to work in every case, a kind of methodological Vaseline which lubricates an entry into the problem and ensures a smooth perfect outcome every time.

A few pages later she re-iterates:

I don't feel at ease with closure, with establishing connections, with setting down the truth with methodological consistency: it's too phallic, too redolent of the old man with the beard giving us the word from the mountain top, engraved in stone. I prefer, or feel compelled, to teeter around on the high heels of ad hoc-istry, bricolaging my arguments, appropriating my paradigms, stumbling blithely from intellectual flower to flower ... Rather than apologizing for my inconsistencies, such as they are, I see them as a major source of strength, as is my lack of a single methodology. [3]

Although Nochlin doesn't use the same terms as most postmodern theorists, she advocates much the same method - avoid any totalising theories at all cost. Her own particular gloss on the question, couched in language I feel quite uneasy about, sets up any attempt to utilise a particular theoretical approach to art history as a masculinist enterprise, akin to rape except that Vaseline is near to hand. Her idea that people try to use a single main method because it's easy and simple and guarantees a perfect outcome every time is a caricature of the efforts of most scholars in the field. I suspect that a few years ago Nochlin would have been quite happy to say that she studied art history using primarily a feminist method, and would not have seen such a stance as 'phallic'.

What does this kind of rejection of so-called totalising theories mean for teaching? Obviously this is a complex question which I cannot address at length here, but I want to look briefly at the example of Edward Said, whose book *Orientalism* has had a huge influence in many fields of culture including art history. Many of us looked again at paintings and photographs of the Middle and near East, newly aware of the discourse of Orientalism which constructed the East as the Other to the Occident. There were no 'ifs', 'buts' or 'may bes' for Said as he wrote 'It is therefore correct that every European, in what he could say about the Orient, was consequently a racist, an imperialist, and almost totally ethnocentric'. [4]

A few years ago, an article on Said as a teacher appeared in the journal of international 'Third World' culture, *Third Text*, number 38, in Spring 1997. Written by Tim Lawrence, this article really surprised me, as it revealed Said to be, in my view, a rather inadequate teacher, who intimidated his students, stormed out of the room in a tantrum and so on. Now admittedly Said is seriously ill, and perhaps this has something to do with some of his actions. Also I recognise that Said, unlike many so-called radical academics, has spoken out about the oppression of the Palestinian people at some risk to himself, so I don't want this to sound like a big anti-Said crusade by an Occidentalist. However, Said's teaching methods described in this article really did sound pretty strange to me. For example he would play Beethoven's music while shouting out pronouncements such as 'There is no longer a powerful coherence, but a sense of fragments left behind. There is no harmonious synthesis.' [5] (We are probably meant to conclude that Beethoven was a post modernist). I could not see any theory, any debate, any testing of anything in this performance, for that is really what it was - a famous scholar giving a performance, presenting himself as a figurehead to be held in awe, perhaps imitated by the brightest and most ambitious of the students.

I later read an interview with Said in which he stated 'I don't see the need for a master discourse or a theorization of the whole.' A few moments later he followed this up with:

I've always thought of my teaching ... as actually performing acts of analysis or reading or interpretation, rather than providing students with methodologies that they can go out and apply to situations.

Said insisted that he didn't do 'encoding insights in some way that can make them useful tools later on. I just don't seem to be able to do that.' [6]

Now admittedly I would be on shaky ground drawing far-reaching conclusions from this one example, but on the strength of this brief look at Said's practice and theory as a teacher, I don't think his particular postmodern academic way of teaching is one that recommends itself. In fact it sounds like quite an old fashioned, academic way of teaching, limited to the seminar room and no use to students who want to go out and apply their knowledge to real situations.

I'd like to propose what I think is a more fruitful approach, which, for the sake of argument, I'll designate 'modernist' and this can be found in the well-known essay by Walter Benjamin, 'The Author as Producer', which was originally given as a talk at the Institute for the Study of Fascism in Paris in April 1934. [7]

I want to draw an analogy with what Benjamin says here (he's talking about creative writing) which would be helpful for thinking about teaching.

An author who teaches writers nothing, teaches no one. What matters, therefore, is the exemplary character of production, which is able first to induce other producers to produce, and second to put an improved apparatus at their disposal. And this apparatus is better the more consumers it is able to turn into producers - that is, readers or spectators into collaborators. [8]

So as a teacher of visual culture history, I would want to do something along the lines that Benjamin suggests for the revolutionary writer. Turn consumers into producers, but not producers of stuff for the same system, using the same means. This is very difficult, and I can't claim that I manage to do this, but really, this is what teaching should do - enable your students to go out and do without you, and, in the end, do it better, contributing to the creation of more critical and radical frameworks of creative knowledge. The present state of education has done much to make children, their parents and students into consumers, in a process which is completely the opposite from the one advocated by Benjamin. Many teachers have reluctantly been forced into the role of stifling what Benjamin calls the 'productive' qualities of children and young students in their care in the interests of the National Curriculum and supposedly raising standards.

I want now to look at a work that, for me, attempts to make its spectator a producer rather than a consumer, and also to consider in what ways we could analyse this work productively, rather than simply giving a performance of analysing it. When I was taught French Literature at University we had to do things called '*explications de texte*' which involved a minute analysis of a fragment of a novel or a poem. This could certainly be intellectually demanding, but did not encourage students to look very far beyond the given text towards its context. The work I've chosen is from a web site by Roshini Kempadoo, entitled 'Sweetness and Light', 1996. I've written and spoken about this image quite a few times, and have decided to do so again because of the ways in which issues of class, 'race' and gender are present in the work. (I am using the term 'race' since I do not accept there is any scientific basis for the division of human beings into groups called races.)

As a Marxist, I have long been interested in issues of class, gender and 'race' and the relationship between these social categories. For years I worked on these topics and suddenly became an interesting commodity to my institution since I was discovered to have skills in researching and publishing which earned my University research points. After twenty-four years at my institution I was promoted to a Chair. Such are the contradictions of higher education under capitalism. I have written extensively on Marxism and art history elsewhere, so I won't go into huge amounts of detail here on what a Marxist art history might be or become. [9] However, I do want to say that it has taken me many years to try and develop a practice of Marxist art history and I think I still have a long way to go. It is not, as Nochlin suggests, an approach which provides an 'easy' guarantee of solving any art historical problem. To describe a Marxist study of visual culture as reductive, economistic, and primarily concerned with a class analysis of art works is really a caricature of what a genuine Marxist approach to culture might be. This implies that Marxists ignore issues of gender and 'race', for example, and also of sexual orientation, at the expense of class. Alas, Tim Clark's famous chapter on Manet's 'Olympia' of 1863, despite being a hugely important milestone in art historical writing, gave a rather skewed view of a Marxist approach (as Clark practised it anyway). For Clark, good paintings really were about class, which was odd, given Clark's rather Hegelian sympathies. However, in his excellent discussion of Manet's picture, Clark wrote: 'I shall end this chapter by arguing that class was the essence of Olympia's modernity and lay behind the great scandal she provoked.' [10]

A Marxist approach to teaching and understanding art history seeks to situate the works in context in a dialectical way, paying attention to ambiguities, contradictions, and tensions, trying to do justice to the totality of cultural and social meanings embodied both consciously and unconsciously in the work. I would agree that the so-called 'economic base' is key here, but that is not the same as trying to show, or believing that, all art works are about class, and the best art works are subtle treatments of class instead of Soviet Socialist Realist paintings.

The title of Roshini Kempadoo's work, 'Sweetness and Light' is also the title of Chapter I of the Victorian scholar Matthew Arnold's book published in 1869, *Culture and Anarchy*. Arnold believed that culture had a political role to play in ameliorating class conflict through improving the human character, especially through a classical education. Kempadoo's web site image, a photographic montage, shows a waitress (posed by the artist herself) serving up on a silver tray a feast of cyberfacts and images, of which we see one - a white man standing in front of a group of black youths in a uniform. Behind this we see the balustrade of a country house garden with a view of its grounds. Emerging from the stonework (and at the same time also disappearing into it) are a series of ethnographic photos of a black woman and a measuring grid. Accompanying the images is a text from a book by William Green on British slavery, and the ways in which slaves were divided into hierarchies of status with house slaves being classified and constructed as more privileged and docile than field slaves. Many English country houses were built with the profits of the slave trade and/or plantations in the West Indies. The classical architecture of the country house is linked to the exploitative relations of 'race', class and gender which underpin them. Kempadoo explains how her work wants to engage with and develop visual and historical analogies - analogies between slavery, plantation production for capitalism, and the new technology information capitalism of the present day. She seeks to make us

Figure 1

Roshini Kempadoo, 'Sweetness and Light', 1996.
Computer-generated colour photographic montage for an Internet Exhibition.
Courtesy of the artist.

question the position of women and black workers in both of these historical moments, not by presenting them separately, but as linked and overlapping with one another.

Another artist who is interested in using new technology in an interactive way, Keith Piper, sees it as a potential means to develop new dialogues around ethnicity and identities:

Racial identities are rapidly evolving, partly caused by technology's role in the production of new images. Take desktop publishing and its promise and, one would hope, fulfilment in enabling a plurality of identities to be heard. On the other hand, access to tools is limited through the means of distribution. That inevitably lies with the large, moneyed institutions. [11]

As the spectator of this work sits at the computer and calls up the web site, Kempadoo seeks to transform her / him from a consumer into a producer, inviting the user to become a historian, a critic, and to become someone equipped to encounter a situation in the high street with a new awareness. This results, as Said put it, in insights 'that can become useful tools later on' though as we have seen he denies that his own work aims to accomplish this. Both Kempadoo and Piper point to the contradictions of technology under capitalism; its liberating potential as well as its use for profit and exploitation. Important in Kempadoo's image is the information 'waitress', and her relation to the image of the woman taken from the ethnographic photograph. The sexual representation and economic exploitation of black women continues, but in different ways. From the house slave, we have moved to the still predominantly female occupations of the nurse, childminder, waitress, cleaner, secretary or call-centre worker. Kempadoo writes:

Conceptualising a 'development' - who, how and by whom can always be seen within a historical framework. As my inevitable exploration of media / cyberspace, information networks and the uses of new technologies takes hold, I begin to look at analogies and comparisons. My thoughts and experiences take me to that of colonialism and the European expansionist past. More specifically, I begin to look at the continuous replication of structures, hierarchies and power bases. I choose to make an analogy - the colonialist experience as characterised by the plantation - whether it is sugar, cotton or cocoa ... The work 'Sweetness and Light' explores some of these thoughts from the position of someone whose ancestry was the 'subject' of the colonial experience. Like all analogies, there are some fundamental differences. So I cannot totally condemn this 'development' of media / cyberspace to a neat and simple comparison. [12]

But if I analyse this work and study its meanings, how do my students know that I am relating theory to practice? I suppose my main answer to this, which some might think rather simplistic, is that I have to tell them this. Theory can't be unconscious if it is to be enabling. Otherwise it's simply ideology or a kind of performance like Said's teaching as described in the *Third Text* article where the students simply don't know what it is they're supposed to be picking up. Nothing is produced, only consumed. [13]

Every analysis of an art work will produce something in the sense that another reading of the work will emerge. But for the reading to be productive in Benjamin's sense it needs to work towards enabling the student / viewer / reader to become productive her / himself, and also 'to put an improved apparatus at their disposal', as Benjamin puts it. Benjamin cites Bertold Brecht's theatre as an example of how an author can change the apparatus with which he works, rather than simply enlivening a derelict one. Brecht's techniques of estrangement and destruction of illusionism result in astonishment and unsettling experiences for the spectator, rather than satisfaction and resolution.

How could this relate to the teaching of art history and visual culture then? How are we to make our students estranged in a productive way rather than satisfied and complacent, when some courses are still taught as if there is a body of knowledge which needs to be transferred from teacher to student, and students are assessed on whether they have assimilated this or not? Postmodern theory is problematic in another way. When Benjamin speaks of Brecht's epic theatre as bringing home 'the real situation' to the spectator, many post modernists would reject such a notion as crude and essentialist. [14]

While 'the real situation' may be complex, ambiguous and contradictory, I would still argue that such a concept as 'the real situation' is valid. Our theoretical frameworks have to be tested out in relation to these real situations. How do we know if our own readings of art works are knowledge or merely discourse? Can cultural theory be what Marxists would term scientific, or is cultural theory the intuitive and sensitive 'other' of a deterministic and rigid method? I believe this false polarisation is an ideological one, which misunderstands the nature of theory and practice in both art and science. In his introduction to the Penguin edition of Marx's *Capital*, volume 1, Ernest Mandel tries to explain Marx's method in researching and understanding capitalism and bourgeois social formations.

In fact, he (Marx) *starts from elements of the material concrete to go to the theoretical abstract, which helps him then to reproduce the concrete totality in his theoretical analysis. In its full richness and deployment, the concrete is always a combination of innumerable theoretical 'abstractions'. But the material concrete, that is, real bourgeois society, exists before this whole scientific endeavour, determines it in the last instance, and remains a constant practical point of reference to test the validity of the theory. Only if the reproduction of this concrete totality in man's thought comes nearer to the real material totality is thought really scientific.* [15]

So I suppose what I am hoping for in teaching art history is the practice of scientific thought, both by me and my students, together with putting into practice key elements of 'The author as producer'. Maybe the key thing at the present time is for us to stop our students remaining consumers within the market of higher education and the low-paid part-time jobs that many of them have to do to pay for their consumerist undergraduate and postgraduate experience. But teaching art history in better ways isn't likely to accomplish that on its own.

References and notes

1   I also recently encountered difficulties supervising an MPhil / Ph.D. student, where it seemed that the fine art supervisor on the team felt that the student was 'doing too much theory', which was inhibiting her ability to develop research in her art practice. Since frameworks for postgraduate research in fine art are still being put in place, the precise relationship of theory to practice remains a site of debate. In any case it should probably vary depending on the individual student and her / his area of study.

2   See for example Bhabha's, *The Location of Culture*. Routledge, 1994. For an excellent critique of Bhabha and other postmodern and post colonial theorists see Ahmad, Aijaz. *In Theory: Classes, Nations, Literatures*. Verso, London, 1992. For a very clear introduction to post colonial criticism and theory see Loomba, A. *Colonialism/Postcolonialism*. Routledge, 1998, and for a contextualisation of the Marxism *vs.* postmodernism debate see Wood, E. M. and Foster, J. B. (Eds.) *In Defence of History: Marxism and the Postmodern Agenda*. Monthly Review Press, New York, 1997.

3   Nochlin, L. *Representing Women*. Thames and Hudson, 1999, pp. 10 & 16.

4   Said, E. *Orientalism*. Penguin Books, 1987, (1978) p. 204.

5   Lawrence, T. 'Edward Said, Late Style and the Aesthetic of Exile', *Third Text*, 38, Spring 1997, pp. 15-24, quote from p. 15.

6   Sprinkler, M. (Ed.) *Edward Said, A. Critical Reader*. Blackwell, 1992, pp. 241 & 248.

7   This essay has been published many times. I used the reprint in Benjamin, W. *Reflections: Essays, Aphorisms, Autobiographical Writings*. Schoken Books, New York, 1986.

8   *Ibid*. p. 233.

9   See my book *Materializing Art History*. Berg, 1998.

10   Clark, T. J. *The Painting of Modern Life: Paris in the Art of Manet and his*

Followers. Thames and Hudson, 1984, p. 88.

11   'The Sample Art of Keith Piper' interview in *Creative Camera*, August-September, 1995, p. 33.

12   Quoted in Willis, D. introduction to *Roshini Kempadoo. Monograph.* Autograph, London, 1997, p. 12. For further discussion of Kempadoo's work, see my *Black Visual Culture: Modernity and Postmodernity*. I. B. Taurus, London, 2000, chapter 2, 'Economics, Histories, Identities'.

13   An interesting issue I do not have time to discuss adequately here is that of 'reading in', and its problems as a teaching model. By this I mean the issue of whether the teacher is providing students with some kind of theory / practice relationship which can be tested in some ways for its historical and scientific validity, or whether the discoveries / knowledges being offered are the product of an individual 'reading in' her / his own particular concerns and interests to an artwork. Clearly both objective and subjective factors come into play in teaching and writing about visual culture. However what balance of these makes a good teaching model? I began to wonder about this after reading a recent book by Griselda Pollock, where she claims that she avoids 'reading in' psycho-biological material in her study of works by women artists such as Artemesia Gentileschi and instead works to 'create a screen for my own, different, feminist desires' by writing about the works. This is not relativism, she argues, but an acknowledgement that what motivates 'reading and interpretation is desire, and that we are responsible for recognising such desire.' *Differencing the Canon: Feminist Desire and the Writing of Art's Histories*. Routledge, London and New York, 1999, pp. 117-119. This clearly opens up some interesting areas of debate, but I wonder how this avoids relativism. And in any case, students have desires and may want to write about their desires rather than the essays their tutors suggest to them. Do we always allow them to do this, and if so, are their articulations of their desires as likely to be published as my own or Griselda Pollock's? Perhaps we art historians ought to consider our own writings more in relation to 'the author as producer' as well as 'the author as desirer'.

14   Benjamin, W. *op. cit.* p. 235.

15   Marx, K. *Capital*, vol 1. introduction by E. Mandel, Penguin, 1976, p. 21.

'Why can't we look at more works by men?': feminism in the classroom.

Rosemary Betterton

Abstract

Feminism has entered the academy with some success over the last twenty five years, not least in the fields of art education - the theories, practices and histories of art. But, what has been the impact of that encounter between a radical political movement, feminism, and a conservative academic discipline, art history? How is the female subject of feminism now positioned, both as lecturer and student? And what responses can we expect from young women and men in the new millennium to feminism in the classroom? This chapter draws on my own experience of the pleasures and perils of teaching gender issues to fine art students at undergraduate and postgraduate levels over a number of years, in order to raise some critical issues facing feminist art history. I shall suggest that feminism has given us certain useful cultural skills, both as theorists and practitioners, before going on to examine some of its negative effects through selected case studies. I shall argue that some current models of feminist art history need to be re-evaluated in the context of the wider shift from the history of art to histories and theories of visual culture.

As Angela McRobbie has suggested, 'when a politics, its theory and aspects of its practice ... meets up with an already existing discipline, the convergence of the two is by no means unproblematic.' [1] In this paper, I want to examine some of the implications for teaching students of the meeting between a radical political movement, feminism, and the traditionally conservative discipline of art history. My intention is neither to offer a historiography of feminist interventions into art history, nor yet to propose an alternative pedagogy, but rather to open up some critical questions around 'teaching feminism' in the classroom which have been left largely unexamined within the discipline. [2] These questions have recently been sharpened for me by a shift in my institutional location from a department of History of Art and Design to an Institute for Women's Studies which has led me to reflect again on some of the tensions and contradictions inherent in the project of a 'feminist' art history.

Feminism in the Academy

As an outsider discourse, one which was initially external to the academy, 'contemporary feminism has been unusually attuned to issues of invisibility and exclusion.' [3] This has particular resonance within the history of art where the issue of visibility - on the walls of museums, in the catalogues of exhibitions, in the pages of books - has been a key issue in the struggle to document, exhibit and write about artworks made by women. Feminist artists, researchers and teachers began the critical work of exposing and articulating the gendered nature of artistic and art historical discourse and, over the last quarter century, have both documented the presence and achievements of women in the arts and developed a substantive critique of their exclusion from the 'canon'. Lynda Nead defines this process in two stages, common to feminist interventions in other fields, the first of which is primarily 'additive', integrating the names and works of women into existing art history, and a second, more critical, stage which seeks to deconstruct the terms of the discipline itself. [4] The effect of this interrogation of art history has been to displace the assumptions of impartial and objective judgement central to the discipline, and to replace them with questions which are both epistemological and ontological in nature: 'What am I looking at and for? What knowledge does my look desire? Who am I when I look at this?' are, as Griselda Pollock suggests, questions 'symptomatic of the encounter between art history and feminism.' [5] Feminism thus challenges the legitimacy of art history by asserting that all knowledge is partial; points of view are always invested with social, political and personal interests and power.

The awareness that we are positioned - both as readers of visual texts and within the power dynamics of institutions - was, as Susan Bordo suggests, 'a cultural moment of revelation and relief', revelation in that it opened up a whole new way of thinking through gender, and relief, in that we found that we were not on our own. [6] As feminists, we could embark on a project that, initially at least, seemed to offer a means of transforming both texts and institutions. I want to locate myself within this account and analyse that moment briefly in terms of my own formation as a feminist academic in order to reflect critically on how my positioning differs from that of students today. I studied art history at Manchester University in the early 1970s in a very traditional department which, typically for the period, was untouched by feminist issues, and where the social history of art was as yet a subversive concept. [7] My engagement with feminist politics came several years later and I found it difficult at first to resolve the tensions between women's movement activism and my new career as an academic. Resolution came through the simultaneous emergence of feminist art history publishing in Britain and a period of intense activity around feminist art practice, exhibitions and conferences at the end of the 1970s and in the early 1980s which enabled me, not without considerable anxieties, to integrate my politics into my teaching for the first time. [8] This was a key moment in my own subject formation as a feminist.

What relevance has this for teaching? Well certainly that my experience is generationally different from that of most of my students today. While students may still engage with feminism as a critical and empowering discourse, they are more likely to encounter it first, not as a form of politics, but as part of their studies, legitimated by rather than outside the academy. Feminist art history is no longer the marginalised discourse that it was in the early 1980s and, indeed, in many ways it has become a key site of academic production. Evidence for this can be seen in the presence of feminist teachers within universities, of gender studies in the curriculum, and in the explosion of feminist research in academic publishing, all of which have effects on how courses are designed and what students now encounter as 'art's histories' within critical studies. [9] There is a recognisable feminist field of study with many diverse and complex theorisations in which, as Gen Doy has shown, analysis no longer focuses exclusively on issues of gender, but engages with difference across other formations of power. But, I want to argue that feminism has been institutionalised in particular forms within the field of art history, in ways which both mark it as part of and as different from the mainstream. [10]

Feminist art historians have undermined the authority of the discipline by revealing it to be a gendered discourse, reading its gendering in specific institutional and textual formations. The central tenets of traditional art history rested on the primacy of the 'masterpiece' and the 'great artist' which served to legitimate ideas of cultural value and meaning. As early as 1971, Linda Nochlin called for a radical feminist critique 'not merely in regard to the question of women artists, but in the formulation of the crucial questions of the discipline as a whole.' [11] The sustained critique of the canon by feminist art historians has shown such concepts of value to be embedded in gendered assumptions (as well as those on those of class and race) in ways which have transformed thinking and teaching about art. But to believe that they have transformed the paradigms of the discipline is to underestimate the power and tenacity of the academy both to resist and incorporate difference. [12] Dominant regimes of knowledge exist not only in relation to their manifest content, but also in the way they organise their field of study. It has proved much more difficult than early critics thought to remap the field of art history, and particularly to dislodge its traditional concerns with the figure of the artist. Perhaps this is not surprising within an art world with vested interests in maintaining the centrality of the individual producer of art, but while the art market and the museum may be the key agents that continue to invest in the concept of the artist, so too does art education. Fine art students are still encouraged to think of themselves first as potential artists rather than as the teachers or mediators of art that they are more likely to become. [13] This presents a paradox for a feminist teacher who may be committed theoretically and politically to deconstructing traditional notions of authorship while, at the same time, finding herself within an institutional context that is premised on those very concepts. This is one reason why, while feminist art histories are no longer characterised by their absence, they have a troubling presence in the academy of art.

Feminism in the Classroom

I want now to consider some of those problems in the context of the classroom, and to pose some questions which have arisen out of my own experience of teaching a second year option entitled 'Gender, Art and the Body' on a Fine Art degree course over a number of years. I am not claiming that I can or should 'teach feminism' as a set of political ideologies, but that feminist analysis can offer crucial theoretical and methodological tools within current fine art practice. As a teacher, I make my own feminist perspective clear to students, but also the need for them to make up their minds about their own position. I am also using the term 'classroom' here intentionally to imply something of the power relations which can be too easily forgotten in the apparent democracy of the seminar (or at least, forgotten by the teacher if not by her students, who have been educated within a system of continuous assessment at school and university). This poses an immediate dilemma for any teacher between the politics of openness on the one hand and her position of power on the other. While this is a dilemma experienced in other disciplines (and not only by feminists), it is perhaps more complicated in art education by the pedagogic relationship between tutor and students which is generally less structured than in lecture-based forms of education.

By exploring the kinds of cultural skills feminism has given to students, I hope to rethink some questions within the field of feminist art history. Like my students, my skills in reading images now are very different from those I had learnt in the 1970s and we can, to some extent, share a set of reading practices. And yet, while I cannot assume that my position as a feminist subject is different from theirs, it does seem to me there is a gap between our assumptions which is exposed in the classroom. It is that 'gap' that I want to think about further here. I am interested in the question of how, as a teacher, I can make connections with students when our experiences of feminism have such different roots and trajectories. [14] What can I expect of them? What do they expect of me?

What I might expect of them is the kind of 'cultural skills' that feminism has taught us: ways of seeing, understanding and representing the world and our location within it through gendered eyes. I am using the term 'cultural skills' here to designate a set of 'practical knowledges' which are impure, a mixture of common and specialist knowledge. Neither methodologically nor theoretically informed, they are nonetheless part of the historically and culturally specific 'baggage' that is taken for granted by educated young women in western societies at the start of the twenty first century. For art students in particular, there are specific visually related skills connected to ways of making and reading images that are only possible as a consequence of three decades of feminist struggle around representation. They include, in no particular order:

- an awareness of how gender shapes looking and the 'gaze'

- a basic understanding of terms like 'gender' and 'patriarchy

- a certain reflexivity in the representation of self

- an ease with collective or group ways of working

- some familiarity with works by women artists

- an ability to read 'against the grain' of a given text.

While this remains at the level of potential rather than actual feminist knowledge unless consciously theorised or analysed historically, I want to suggest that most, if not all, of my students are fairly proficient in these sort of cultural skills. I should say that, as with any option, it is in the nature of students to be self selecting; the majority of these are women, but only a small minority would identify themselves as feminists, more often than not these are mature students. So, if this is what I can expect, what can I offer them?

- some methodological tools for an analysis of gender in representation

- an understanding of a range of theoretical perspectives

- knowledge of relevant critical and artistic histories of cultural production

- an awareness of precedents which can help to situate their own practice

- support in defining their own ideas about gender issues

- a context in which they can explore issues of gender and sexuality

- recognition of the affective dimensions of study.

The last three points are perhaps most specific to feminist pedagogy and I've found them to be significant in relation to those least supported within art education, students who are lesbians or mothers, some of whom only identify themselves as such in the course of their final year. Whether or not I can deliver on these expectations is a separate question. But I want now to identify some of the issues arising out of them.

Charlotte Brunsdon has characterised the complex responses of students to her teaching on 'women's genres' in film and television as a mixture of: 'disruption, disappointment and deference.' [15] Although the issues raised in teaching material on representations of the body within fine art practices are very different, I want to adapt her terms to explore a range of student responses to looking at visual images. To deal with deference first, which may seem the least problematic. By this I mean when students accept feminist readings of texts uncritically even where, as it subsequently appears in discussion, these readings do not correspond to their own responses. Students may defer to feminist textual readings for a number of reasons. They may genuinely be engaged by them as explanations, but alternatively they may be bored or uninterested, or simply want to please the tutor. The problem this generates for teaching is one of preconceived opinions, students often already understand what positions they are expected to adopt as readers. This is particularly the case in relation to the study of the nude where the feminist literature in the field is well-established, but the debates, while increasingly theoretically sophisticated, do not occupy a wide range of critical positions. It may therefore be difficult to generate real discussion about an image, because students think they already 'know' what they are supposed to think about the female nude and the male gaze. A case in point would be Manet's 'Olympia', where readings which were once radical have become orthodox.

Compared to students reading in terms of an assumed 'correct' response, the second kind of reaction: a refusal to read images at all in terms of gender, is more straightforwardly disruptive. This disruption may occur in a number of ways: in the form of non-attendance or maintaining silence in seminars; in direct confrontations with the tutor, or in an attempt to redress what is perceived to be the 'bias' of teaching: 'Why can't we look at more work by men?' I suggest that this stems from the common perception of feminism as being 'anti-men', a comment which is made by both male and female students. This may, in part at least, be justified by the way in which some feminist critics appear to adopt an accusatory stance towards their subjects. There is a tendency within some versions of feminist art history to demonise the 'great' male artist - Van Gogh, Jackson Pollock - and conversely to make women artists into victims or heroines - Frida Kahlo or Louise Bourgeois. I do not find myself often in agreement with Paul Wood, but I do agree with his critique of a certain type of moralising art history which belittles its subject from 'a desire to unmask it as a creature of sundry bourgeois and patriarchal ideologies.' [16] While it is essential to challenge art history's own mythologies, simply to reverse them in gender terms is both intellectually unproductive and creates problems for the student in the classroom. To cite one example is probably unfair, but I shall do it anyway. In Jo Anna Isaak's essay, 'Art History and its (Dis)Contents' [1996], she discusses Matisse's relation to his models in the series of Odalisque paintings he produced in the interwar period in Nice. Quite rightly, she locates these paintings within the context of 'fashionable colonial discourse' in the wake of France's national defeat in WW1. She also quotes a letter from Matisse to his son written in 1940:

I've arranged with an agency for film extras to send me their prettiest girls. The ones I don't use I pay off with 10 francs. Thanks to this system I have three or four young and pretty models. I have them pose in shifts, for sketching, three hours in the morning, three hours in the afternoon. And this keeps me in the studio.

Matisse's attitude to his models in 1940 is pretty cavalier, but it does not constitute a basis for reading his 1926 'Odalisque' as 'a site of acute discomfort' for the model. [17] It rather prompts other questions I'd want to ask - and encourage students to ask - for example, about the failure of a certain myth of artistic masculinity in Matisse's old age, or even about the conditions of female working class employment in occupied France in which modelling or work as a film extra might well be preferable to domestic service or prostitution. This form of feminist 'political correctness' can provoke a defensive or disruptive response.

The third, and to me most interesting, response is disappointment, that visual texts claimed to be 'feminist' do not somehow deliver such meanings for the student or, conversely that works which the student holds dear can be dismissed within feminist criticism. I am often struck by the gap between feminist critical readings of art works and student responses to them. What concerns me is the disjuncture between textual readings informed by increasingly complex theoretical frameworks and their different readings by students. How do we account for these differences? According to an 'expert' reading, by which I mean one informed by knowledge of relevant history and theory as well as sophisticated decoding skills, the student response is seen as misinformed or incomplete, to be discounted as irrelevant and culturally incompetent. But what is foreclosed is precisely the questions of who is looking and what they are looking for. As Brunsdon suggests, this is 'experientially and theoretically complicated if questions of participants' very identity are conceptually at stake', as is often the case when addressing issues of the body and sexuality where personal meanings for individuals may be intense. [18] I want to use as an example of this, two readings of works by Toulouse-Lautrec, one by Griselda Pollock and the other in a student essay. What happens when a woman reads 'against the grain' of a feminist reading? In Pollock's recent book, *Differencing the Canon: Feminist Desire and the Writing of Art's Histories* [1999], she has a section entitled 'Cocking A Leg at Toulouse-Lautrec', with a series of witty subtitles which include 'Late-coming and premature departure' and 'When small is not enough', intended to debunk the modernist mythology of the sexually potent male artist. She offers a fascinating psychoanalytic reading of Lautrec's work as 'psychically impotent', including an analysis of his representation of lesbian love-making in maisons closes, the regulated brothels in late nineteenth century Paris, of which she comments:

I find these images hard to look at. They were probably the product of Toulouse-Lautrec's money buying the spectacle of lesbian love-making as part of the erotic services women were paid to perform in a brothel. The images are painted for some man who will occupy the place the artist used to sketch the subject, if not to execute the final painting. They make women's sexual pleasure and intimacy yet another voyeuristic commodity. [19]

I do not want to argue with Pollock's reading, but simply to set it against that of a student who chose to look at the same images in an essay. For the student, Lautrec's paintings offered a totally different set of meanings which she saw as validating her own lesbian identity as well as offering a rare and sympathetic representation of active lesbian sexuality. Rather than assuming her naivety, I want to suggest instead that her response should be seen as proceeding from a different set of experiences and knowledges from that of Pollock's, a difference which may open up a productive space in which to explore questions of how meanings are made and for whom. While we offer ever more sophisticated readings of artworks informed by psychoanalysis or semiotics, we have little knowledge of how and why 'actual' viewers of images understand them. This is not an argument for less careful attention to texts as signifiers of meaning, but rather that, as feminists, we also need to attend more to women as viewers of images and the knowledge they produce about them.

The implications for the teaching of feminist art histories would be a shift away from the paradigms of art history towards those undertaken by radical approaches in other fields of feminist enquiry, from traditional concerns with the artist-text relationship to attention to the multiple inscriptions of women as the subjects of spectatorship. The concept of 'visual culture' implies this broader project of analysing representations and responses to them across a range of visual practices, but Hal Foster poses pertinent questions when he asks: 'Is visual culture only a surrogate for a retooled modernism, a revised art history, a redesigned museum? Or is it a placeholder for new formations not yet defined?' [20] Little will change if the term is used to rename flagging departments of art history, an institutional realignment which allows the issues of power and authorisation at stake in the discourse to remain hidden. But if, visual culture is to respond to 'new formations not yet defined', then feminist analysis, because it interrogates relations of power, will be crucial to the questions visual culture asks of itself and others.

References and notes

1   McRobbie, A. 'The politics of feminist research: between talk, text and action', *Feminist Review*, 1982, p. 46.

2   For a discussion of these issues in relation to film and media studies, see Brunsdon, C. 'Pedagogies of the feminine: feminist teaching and women's genres', *Screen,* 32:4, Winter 1991, and Williamson, J. 'How does girl number twenty understand ideology?', *Screen Education*, 40, 1981-82.

3   Bordo, S. 'Feminism, postmodernism and gender scepticism' in Nicolson, L. (Ed.) *Feminism/Postmodernism.* 1990, p. 141.

4   Nead, L. 'Feminism, Art history and Cultural Politics' in Borzello, F. & Rees, A. L. (Eds.) *The New Art History.* Camden Press, 1986.

5   Pollock, G. 'What Difference Does Feminism Make to Art History?' in R. Kendall & G. Pollock (Eds.) *Dealing With Degas: Representations of Women and the Politics of Vision.* Pandora, 1992, p. 36. Susan Bordo asks similar questions of philosophy: '*Whose* truth? *Whose* nature? *Whose* version of reason? *Whose* history? *Whose* tradition?' Bordo, S. *op. cit,* 1990, p. 137.

6   Bordo, S. 1990, *Ibid.*

7   It is ironic that I was taught briefly by Marcia Pointon, now a noted feminist scholar and just missed being taught by Griselda Pollock.

8   These include Petersen, K. & Wilson, J. J. *Women Artists.* 1978, The Women's Press; Greer, G. *The Obstacle Race.* 1979, Picador; and Parker, R. & Pollock, G. *Old Mistresses: Women, Art and Ideology.* RKP, 1981. Exhibitions include the three shows, 'Images of Men', 'About Time' and 'Issues', at the Institute of Contemporary Arts, London in 1980 and various conferences organised in connection with the Women Artist's Slide Library and the journal, *Feminist Art News.*

10 See Doy, G. *Materializing Art History.* Berg Publishers, 1999, and Pollock, G. *Avant-Garde Gambits 1888-1893. Gender and the Colour of Art History.* Thames and Hudson, 1992.

11   Nochlin, L. 'Why have there been no great women artists' in T. B. Hess & E. C. Baker (Eds.) *Art and Sexual Politics.* Collier Macmillan, 1973, p. 2.

12   As Lynda Nead warned in 1986: 'Meaning is produced in terms of difference and feminism has to resist becoming a term of difference for the traditional discipline.' Borzello, F. & Rees, A. L. (Eds.) *The New Art History.* 1986, p. 120, or as Adrian Rifkin put it in the same volume, 'feminism may be taken on as an option in the 'new' art history, but '(t)he masterpieces stay put.' 1986, p. 162.

13   HESA has recently published statistics that show Fine Art students have the highest percentage of employment six months after graduation of any subject area, as reported in the *Guardian Higher*, 18.1.2000, p. 3.

14   This was brought home to me by a woman student working on a feminist dissertation topic who nevertheless identified feminism with her mother's generation and saw it in largely negative, stereotypical terms.

15   Brunsdon, C. [1991] *op. cit.* p. 373.

16   Wood, P. 'Picasso in Words' *Art History,* Vol. 21, No. 3. September 1998, p. 432.

17   All quotations are taken from Isaak, J. A, *Feminism and Contemporary Art: the Revolutionary Power of Women's Laughter.* Routledge, 1996, p. 59.

18   Brunsdon, C. [1991] *op. cit.* p. 375.

19   Pollock, G. *Differencing the Canon: Feminist Desire and the Writing of Art's Histories.* Routledge, 1999, p. 88.

20   Foster, H. 'The Archive without Museums', *October*, Summer 1996, 77, p. 100.

Out of Service: Art History in Art Education

Marsha Meskimmon

Abstract

Residual tensions between art history and art practice are exacerbated by the teaching and learning models still operative in many institutions. At worst, art history functions as a subsidiary form of service teaching, enabling practitioners to write the few, unimportant words of their dissertations and artist-statements in order to pass their degrees. Using this paradigm, art history stands isolated from practice as a dull, stagnant discipline - a parasite on making. This chapter looks at this problem directly and suggests alternate versions of disciplinary dialogue by which both art practice and art history are enriched by their exchanges. I would like to suggest that art history can be as vital a disciplinary area for makers as it is for cultural historians and theorists and, moreover, that art historians and practitioners can learn from one another to develop more holistic approaches to forms of research which are both visual and textual.

Out of Service: inoperative debate

It had been my intention to address the problematic relationship between the discipline of art history and current forms of art education in the United Kingdom by arguing that the present state of play was still misinformed by a model of 'service teaching' and that the potential for more productive interaction could only come through alternative forms of dialogue between the areas. I still wish to argue the latter point, and at some length, in the second part of this chapter, but the starting point now seems to reside before and beyond the 'service teaching' model.

As a service teaching activity, art history provides practitioners with information about the historical development of their discipline, fine art, along with a variety of remedial writing skills and a general critical framework through which to explore making and meaning. What is excluded from this model is the historiography of art history as a discipline itself - its origins, internal conflicts and contemporary theoretical paradigms. Those artists and students who come across the discipline in its service-teaching capacity have every right to think that art history is dull, staid and élitist not to mention a parasite on making, since this form of activity only operates in the wake of practice, as its handmaiden or judge.

The trouble is, this version of art history *isn't*. Within art education, art history as a discipline in its own right has little provision and even less good will; studio practitioners pressed for curricular time do not want to waste it on an antiquated, irrelevant subject and art historians, often their own worst enemy, feel their area to be too difficult and specialist to explain to 'mere' makers. Even if these entrenched positions can continue to offer a model of accommodation between art practice and art history within institutions, they will not lead to positive new models of inter-disciplinary praxis. To do so means to take seriously, as the title of this series suggests, disciplines, fields and change in art education. Hence, a brief discussion of the historical, theoretical and institutional development of art history as a discipline is a useful starting point toward a more fruitful pedagogical dialogue between art practice and art history.

Art history's status as an academic subtext was won much later than other arts and humanities areas, such as philosophy, history, classics and literature, and its links with both the art market and matters of taste and connoisseurship have always plagued its scholarly claims. Many of the earliest writings now taken to have founded art history are concerned with elevating the status of art, artists and 'men' of taste. During the period of the Italian Renaissance, for example, artists and scholars argued forcibly for the acceptance of painting and sculpture into the higher realm of the Liberal Arts, while during the course of the eighteenth and nineteenth centuries, élitism was sustained through the image of the cultured 'man', capable of judging the value of objects and images. This 'higher' function of embryonic art historical praxis was accompanied by the rise of the art market and the art historian's role as an authenticator and adjudicator of the value (financial and aesthetic) of works of art.

If, however, art history went hand-in-hand with class, status, patronage and the power of taste and connoisseurship, it also had a special relationship with politics, social history and the 'stuff' of the past. Toward the latter half of the nineteenth century, the scholarly discipline of art history began to emerge from within archaeology through arguments asserting that specialist research and methodologies were needed to understand that class of ancient artefacts better termed 'art'. From this early research, principally concerned with the art and architecture of the classical past, came studies of iconography, style, patronage and periodisation which would inform the discipline variously throughout the twentieth century. During the course of the 1930s, the academic discipline of art history received renewed impetus from politicised scholars who argued effectively that the study of art history was a crucial element within the humanities since it had the possibility of explaining cultural change in truly novel ways. In no part was art history, as conceived by these scholars, a peripheral, subjective pursuit to be undertaken by those wishing to acquire good taste.

Remarkably similar claims for the scholarly status of art history were voiced during the 1970s and 1980s when the discipline underwent a series of challenges from within as it responded to the socio-political perspectives of what is now broadly designated as 'critical theory'. The complacency of art history with regard to its canon of masters, its relegation of whole realms of visual material to obscurity, its ignorance of its own inherent gender, national and racial biases and its reliance upon simplistic theories of authorship for interpretation, came under attack in this period. For many reasons, I would affirm the rejection of connoisseurship in favour of understanding art historical research as an important part of a more inclusive, cross-disciplinary form of humanities scholarship, not least because we live in and produce an increasingly visual culture which should not be left without critique or comment. However, there is an interesting residual tension within art history as a discipline wholly conceived through its connections with the humanities, since to maintain its objective, academic status within this remit, it has often effaced its vital connections with art practice.

If we explore the current institutional framework within which teaching and research in art history are pursued in the UK, this problematic is revealed very clearly. There is a marked split between art history departments residing within humanities faculties which have no connection to art practice and art history departments with integral links to fine art departments. This division corresponds very closely to the division between the 'pre-1992' ('old') Universities and the 'post-1992' ('new') Universities, with a few noteworthy exceptions such as the flourishing art and art history departments in Leeds, Reading and Goldsmiths, not to mention the recent mergers in Southampton and Loughborough between former monotechnics and pre 1992 Universities, which have formed a new hybrid type.

However, these few exceptional cases merely prove the rule; art history's institutional placement within higher education remains polarised in ways which affect the development of the discipline. The results for art and design history in the 1996 Research Assessment Exercise (RAE) demonstrate this point very well. Of the 45 entries into the assessment, 19 were graded between 4 and 5 (the highest being 5). This represents approximately 45 percent of the entries and, regardless of the efficacy of the RAE as a means by which research can be assessed more generally, indicates very clearly that the discipline is a formidable research power by institutional standards in Britain. Yet, of the 19 highly-rated departments, only one was in a 'new' University (though Leeds and Reading fell into this band). By complete contrast, of the 26 entries within the lower bands (1, 2, 3b, 3a), 19 were from 'new' Universities or monotechnics.

Again I must emphasise that I do not look to the results of the RAE to demonstrate quality thinking and scholarship among individuals, but rather to indicate institutional hierarchies and economic privilege within the disciplinary area, and I also recognise that the 2001 RAE may well provide some significant shifts in the power bases within art history. Still, the 1996 results are indicative of a disciplinary divide. Where art history was least associated with practice and contemporary topics, both in terms of teaching and research, it reaped rewards. Opportunities to do research within any field are linked to fewer teaching hours, research leave and financial assistance, not to mention the chance to teach within your research specialisms, supervise postgraduate students and challenge the discipline itself within your pedagogical praxis. In general, all of these opportunities for art historians are increased if they turn their back on service-teaching and reside almost wholly within the pre-1992 sector. If the level of art history being taught to practitioners is poor, it is a systemic problem; if the central concerns of art history are removed from those of art practice, it is hardly surprising given the institutional pressures splitting the discipline.

This is the wider context through which I feel we can move forward to address art history in art education more fully and with more sensitivity to reciprocal interaction at all levels. We cannot proceed by taking the service-teaching model as representative of the discipline, either institutionally or in terms of advanced scholarly interventions. We must bring the more complete picture to the debate.

Out of Service: from servitude to dialogue

Within art education at higher degree level in the UK, art history figures as a key component in course programmes and as the focus of much discussion in terms of curricular development. Yet it commonly stands outside the core learning activities of practice-based students as an 'other' with which they must contend. Genuine inter-disciplinary activity is rare and the preferred mode of contact remains a form of accommodation between two areas presumed to be at odds at a fundamental level.

In part, this is simply a matter of semantics, of the ways core activities are defined. Artists, as students and as professionals, engage in practice; art historians, as both students and professionals, conduct research. There is a great need within art education to explore the connections between these two modes more closely. Institutionally however, these differences have been exacerbated by the increasing weight of governmental monitoring such as the ESR and the RAE which attempt to codify the nature of the activities taking place within Higher Education for the purposes of allocating (read: cutting) funds. But the nature of learning and scholarship cannot be reduced to fit into the boxes on a proforma in triplicate. Enforcing a linguistic distinction between practice and research so that the activities of artists and art historians might better be understood is absurd. It has, if anything, increased the divide.

Furthermore, many artists and art historians themselves now conceive research and practice in oppositional terms and find themselves placed oppositionally within institutional structures. I myself have been party to numerous, heated debates concerning institutional definitions of 'research' which were argued to be wholly unsympathetic to 'practice'. Rather than seeking links and new ways of thinking about structures, accepting this dichotomy reinforces a binary split to which we become resigned. It is at this point that the wider framework of art history as a research and teaching activity within the UK becomes significant since art history as a discipline under the umbrella of the humanities can be defined very easily and clearly within the contemporary constructs of 'research'. Therefore, art historians within fine art departments need not clash with the prevailing structures of disciplinary definition in the way that their studio colleagues must; art historians need only to turn from practice, toward the other pole within their own discipline - namely humanities-based art history - to succeed in the current climate.

Self-reflection within art history is often one-sided for just this reason. While institutional pressures were brought to bear on art history to define itself as an active and relevant research area within the humanities, rather than an élitist amateur pursuit associated with connoisseurs, no similar pressure has been exerted to think through the discipline's dynamic relationship with art-making. And, while I would applaud the exceptionally high level of inter-disciplinary scholarship in 'humanities' art history, I feel that the discipline's ignorance of practice comes at great cost to itself. What follows are some collected thoughts on links between the activities and processes of art historical research and art practice and the ramifications these might have for more holistic pedagogical methods within art history as a participant in art education. In thinking about this, I am indebted to both the research and scholarship within art history which has allowed it to forge integral bonds with disciplines such as philosophy, history, literature and the social sciences and to the tremendous theoretical moves made within recent art practice. My aim is to bring the best of both together, rather than to replicate the stalemate propounded by institutions and normative thinking.

Research and Practice: making meanings

Significantly, working toward more fulsome dialogues between art history and art-making does not mean collapsing their differences into some form of over-general meta-narrative. Productive inter-disciplinary scholarship need not assimilate the particular knowledges and insights of different areas into one, basic 'truth'; rather, it can build bridges and lines of connection between disparate ideas and materials so that reconfigurations of meaning may be brought into view. While I will argue against the simplistic binary division between 'research' and 'practice', citing their crossing points as providing alternative models of activity, I do not see art history and art practice as the same.

The reason for attending to these differences might be made more clear by analogy. In examining culture, in the anthropological use of that term, certain paradigms emphasise the deep and underlying structural sameness between all human cultures, from all places and in all times. But such models say less about 'cultures' than they do about instinctual processes. In order to find these universal structures, local and temporal differences in behavioural patterns must be effaced with the resultant effect that the remaining similarities are so general as to be meaningless. That is, accounting for cultural difference in terms of the basic human drives to feed, fornicate, fight and flee, does not explain the sophisticated negotiation between individuals within particular groups exploiting specific environmental constraints. Saying that a Chinese man living during the period of the Ming Dynasty, an aboriginal woman from Papua New Guinea and I all eat, says nothing.

I wish to avoid trivialising the connections between art history and art practice in this chapter through recourse to reductive definitions of a similar sort and to emphasise instead the active links that can be made in specific areas and instances. Moreover, I want to suggest that these connections are not eternal - that the relationships between theory and practice require constant dialogue and re negotiation. Thus, art history is not art-making and research is not practice; rather, art historians and artists can (and do) engage with both modes, combining, critiquing and configuring them in many productive ways.

It is perhaps the 'products' of art history and art practice which are most different, and a crude focus on results, typical of institutional monitoring of subject areas and their activities, causes tensions to erupt between practice and research. Research 'outcomes', as defined by monitoring agencies, seem straightforward: they consist of a number of standard publication forms from single-authored monographs to articles, essays and reviews. For art historians, the only significant challenge appears when the public result of research is in the form of an exhibition and in these instances, the verifiable outcome is usually taken to be the catalogue. For practitioners, these outcomes are far more problematic. What do practitioners make? What does art-making mean?

If art-making is taken to mean the production of inert objects which contain that essence which is 'art', then practice is entirely about the manual processes of making (art) things. In this sense, it does not fit any institutional definitions of 'research' and it cannot connect, in its intrinsic form, with art history and theory. It is at odds with 'research'. But artists make far more than this when they engage in art practice. Artists make meanings, they develop symbols, they figure ideas, they define spaces and they produce knowledges. Making 'art' is a dialogic process which opens up a circulation between visuality, materiality, thought and articulation. Moreover, the intrinsic emphasis upon process in art-making refutes the residual claim that art is contained by objects, themselves the result of mute, uni-directional, manual labour. Practice may be resistant to the dull expectation of codifiable outcomes fostered by the present institutional structures, but it is not closed to dialogues with art history and theory in its methods or its manifestations; in its fascinating combination of research and practice, it moves beyond oppositional polarities.

Attention's Loop: A Sculptor's Reverie on the Coexistence of Substance and Spirit, a small volume recently published by the US sculptor Elizabeth King, demonstrates the valuable connections which can be made between art history and art-making by a practitioner. King never reduces the specificity of her making processes, or assimilates the variety of her thinking and working methods, to a unitary paradigm of 'research'. Instead, the volume displays the lateral moves made between conventional, even traditional, historical research, personal memory, myth, scientific and technical invention and her own material practice as a figurative sculptor.

Attention's Loop is in itself an exquisite object, combining beautiful black and white photographs of a small, sculptural self-portrait of the author (Figure 1), with texts

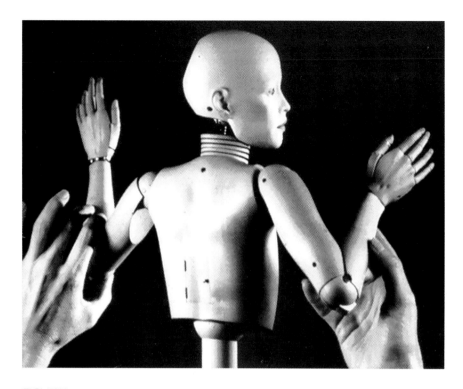

FIGURE 1

Elizabeth King
'Pupil'/Attention's Loop, 1999
Figure posed by artist.
By kind permission of Elizabeth King, photograph by Katherine Wetzel.

and graphics designed to enhance the aesthetic experience of reading the work (See Figures 1 and 2 overleaf). Pages (in the original) are laid out in a subtle monochrome palette, such that the photographs, taken by Katherine Wetzel, seem to change in tone and timbre along with the different stories and voices in the texts.

As a child in Michigan I once had a small bean: an amulet made of some kind of hollowed shell, about the size and shape of a navy bean. It had a lid with a tiny knob on it, and when you uncorked it you could shake out onto your palm twelve ivory (ivory!) elephants. [1]

FIGURE 2

Elizabeth King
'Pupil'/Attention's Loop, 1999
Looking at hand gesture (placed opposite the Bean Story)
By kind permission of Elizabeth King, photograph by Katherine Wetzel.

My friend Myron complains that I constantly interrupt him ... I insist that my mind is working topologically and interruption isn't a change of subject as he thinks but rather an increasing number of things being discussed simultaneously. [2]

FIGURE 3

Elizabeth King
'Pupil'/Attention's Loop, 1999
Hand close-up 'Interruptions' By kind permission of Elizabeth King, photograph by
Katherine Wetzel.

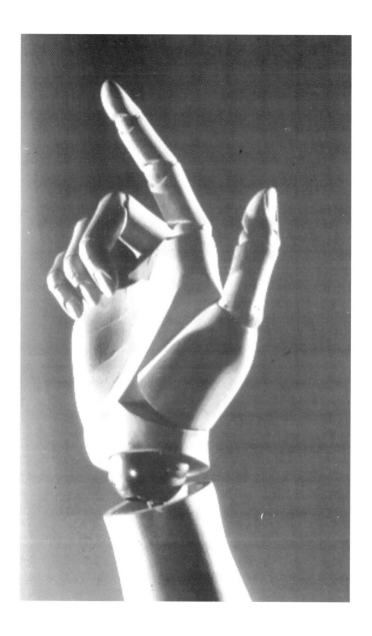

It is the sort of volume you might imagine a sculptor would produce, and its tactility is striking, yet it is not confined by its distinct appeal to its readers as an object alone.

King's book works with the metaphor of the 'loop' or 'round-trip' journey, suggesting that there is no necessary, or singular, point of entry into the volume. Like the images found throughout the pages, the textual material is diverse and operates through different voices and tones. There are sections devoted to art-historical survey material - the Renaissance and Baroque traditions of portrait sculpture and the difficulty of producing self-portraits - and there are passages which trace historical, literary and folkloric descriptions of the making of figures - sixteenth century clock-making and automata, Tom Thumb and the Golem. Etymology (such as a key passage on the word 'pupil', which is the title of King's figure) and scientific explorations (e.g. developments in reproductive technologies) are yet more textual voices echoing in the text.

These various threads are pulled together through their connections with vital narratives of living and making art which punctuate the volume at key points:

As a child in Michigan I once had a small bean: an amulet made of some kind of hollowed shell, about the size and shape of a navy bean. It had a lid with a tiny knob on it, and when you uncorked it you could shake out onto your palm twelve ivory (ivory!) elephants. [1] (See Figure 2)

My friend Myron complains that I constantly interrupt him ... I insist that my mind is working topologically and interruption isn't a change of subject as he thinks but rather an increasing number of things being discussed simultaneously. [2] (See Figure 3)

Some of the most striking sections of the text are passages devoted to describing the interaction between eye, mind and hand in the studio as work is made. Here, in the processes of making - making the 'self', making 'art', making the self as art - the loops of the volume are able to correspond, reiterate and open outward. A lengthy passage headed as 'Cascade' shows this circulation of making and thinking:

Work proceeds as a series of self-interruptions. For example, you take a small block of wood to the bandsaw to cut it into a stack of thin layers. But first you have to make a jig to hold the block ... You make an unnecessarily elegant jig, in private indulgence ... You think forward and move backward ... Yes, drill the hole before cutting the slats. Should the hole be in the center? ... You think backward and move forward: this time I'm going to make the joints from scratch. [3]

King's art-making integrates 'research' and 'practice', producing a dynamic space in which meanings are made across disciplinary boundaries through 'topological interruptions'. The lateral connections never efface the different voices within the volume and the objects and images maintain their particular capacities to move us - they are not 'explained' by the texts.

Such a model has pedagogical implications for art history within art education, since it brings traditional strands of humanities research into close contact with practice by emphasising the processes (read, lived, seen, touched, performed) by which their relationship is continually refigured. It suggests that art history is not an imposition from outside, but part of the shared space of art- and meaning-making. For art historians teaching studio practitioners, the development of a space in which specialist knowledges can be shared toward creative ends, means that both the artists and the historians must be willing to learn from one another. This risks reversing the conventional teacher-student hierarchy and questions the efficacy of a fully humanities-based art history. To over-simplify, if artists can make all forms of research integral to their practice, can art historians make practice a vital element in art historical research?

As the above passages suggest, I suspect there are a number of extra-disciplinary issues at stake in considering changing art history by its contact with practice, not least the trajectory of the discipline within institutional frameworks which support research. The potential loss of status accompanied by acknowledging a form of making to be intrinsic to intellectual pursuits should not be discounted either. We are all familiar with the disciplinary hierarchies which eschew manual labour, the taint of corporeality or sensual, subjective perspectives, defining these as beyond rational thought. Art historians working with scholars in the humanities are easily made to seem peripheral, decorative or less rigorous in their scholarship because they are concerned with art (and I am all too aware that these are also features cast in the 'feminine' in order to marginalise them further). To argue that there are important connections between practice and art history, and that academics might learn from artists, is a dangerous premise. [4]

Yet disconnecting academic work on art from the making of works has led to some disastrous results. Mira Schor, in the preface to her volume of collected essays, *Wet: On Painting, Feminism and Art Culture*, tackles this directly. As a practitioner and theorist, she finds that much feminist theoretical work which ostensibly speaks to painting, actually says nothing about the medium. In a very long footnote, for example, she writes of her disappointment when, seeing the sub-title of an essay by a prominent British feminist philosopher, 'Irigaray, Painting and Psychoanalysis', she read the article only to find it was at best, ignoring painting and at worst, ignorant of painting. [5]

Schor argues consistently throughout her diverse work that theoretical issues emerge and open themselves to questions from attention to art. This is not the same as describing works or practices, nor does it mark a return to connoisseurship or unthinking formalism. Rather, Schor's position echoes that of the graphics historian Kathryn Reeves, who argues convincingly that histories of printmaking are either dominated by technical description which effaces thoughtful analysis of the processes involved, or by historical surveys written by people who do not know of or understand those self-same processes. [6] To discuss the radical potential of printmaking without knowing the difference between an etching and a lithograph might seem beyond belief, but it certainly happens.

I would argue that there are two opportunities being lost by art historians unwilling to engage with art practice and that each of these can speak to a re-thought pedagogy. First, at an obvious level, ignorance of the materials and methods of practitioners makes it impossible to engage fully with their work. On a scholarly level, we might raise the question of rigour in this sense. If an art historian will study the letters, manifestos, critical surveys and theoretical texts produced by and about an artist or group of artists, why would they not investigate artists' working methods, processes and techniques? How can we begin to share a productive pedagogical space with our studio students when we make it clear that their material investigations are of no interest to us when we speak of art?

The second missed opportunity is less obvious, but equally pervasive. The conceit at the heart of most conventional forms of art history is that art historians are objective interpreters of art; that art historical discourse is a transparent 'reading' of works which open themselves as objects to the distanced, knowing subject. If, however, art history is rethought as being itself a practice (not art practice), we can begin to ask far more exciting questions of the discipline. What, for example, do practising art historians make? How are they involved in and changed by this making process and, how do they negotiate the relationship between text, image and object, so fundamental to art history? While 'answering' these questions is, of course, part of the process of renewal and thus never able to be completed, positing just a few ideas around these areas will suffice to show how dynamic art history becomes when it envisages itself differently. Acknowledging an intimacy with visual and material culture, for example, refutes interpretative models based on translation or assimilation in favour of active exchange. The corporeal address of art will not be reduced to text, but art historians using this paradox (rather than attempting to hide it) can bridge multiple modes of making and knowing in their writing and thinking. Art history acts as a pivot between text-based theoretical discourses and the varied languages of art, by knowing their histories and postulating their connections.

Pedagogically, art historians can and do operate at the interstices between traditional academic disciplines and art practice, making each more available to the other. This activity becomes increasingly important as the critical function of so-called visual and material cultures in contemporary society is recognised. If the 'makers' of visual culture are divorced from the consumers/critics of their production, distressing alienation will follow.

The art historian, as well as building bridges, makes contexts and histories. Works of art are made visible by the actions of art historians, producing constellations of ideas, objects, images, texts, facts, interpretations, theories and practices. Art history does not immaterially reflect history, it corporeally produces it. In this way, it is a key component of the creation of aesthetic spaces and modes of reading, seeing and touching artworks, not just a passive mirror to their meanings.

As a final pedagogical move, I merely refer to a degree course currently in its third year at my own institution, Loughborough University, which we have called 'History of Art and Design with Studio Practice'. While this programme is really in its infancy, and certainly continuing to undergo teething problems, it has produced one fascinating effect which none of us on the teaching team had ever expected.

The programme is not a joint-honours degree in art history and practice; it is a single honours degree in art and design history which utilises the hands-on experience of studio work as a pedagogical technique for the training of art historians. In practical terms, all students spend one day each week in studios undertaking a combination of tasks from life drawing to preliminary printmaking, photography and 3-D work. As the course progresses over three years, they are encouraged to specialise in areas which they feel complement their theoretical and historical work best. Some, keenly interested in feminist theory and the body, for example, have devoted long hours to paper-making and latex body-casting over the past year.

We also run a joint honours programme in art history combining it with English and Drama. These students, as joint honours candidates, do not do studio work, but undertake all lecture-based (historical and theoretical) modules in addition to their package with English and Drama. What we have now found as a consistent student perspective is that the English and Drama joint honours students feel that they cannot do art historical work as well as their colleagues attending studio modules, because they are without the intimate connection with practice. We have now had to make provision for these students to audit studio courses in their own time. Far from finding that art history is complete when it is connected only to humanities research, these students suggest that the link with practice is crucial. Those links need to be explored, developed and made more vital to art history, just as art history can be intrinsic to innovative making.

References and notes

1   King, Elizabeth. *Attention's Loop: A Sculptor's Reverie on the Coexistence of Substance and Spirit*. New York: Harry N. Abrams Inc., 1999, p. 22.

2   *Ibid*. p. 74.

3   *Ibid*. p. 32.

4   Barbara Stafford even goes so far as to say that our knowledge structures are so bound to textuality that they refute the insistent claims of the visual full stop. See Stafford, B. *Good Looking: Essays on the Virtue of Images*. Cambridge, MA: MIT Press, 1996.

5   Schor, Mira. *Wet: On Painting, Feminism and Art Culture*. Durham, NC and London: Duke University Press, 1997, p. 216 [note 5].

6   Reeves, Kathryn. 'Printed Matter(s)', in *Relativities: The Fourth British International Miniature Print Exhibition*. Mike North (Ed.) Loughborough University School of Art and Design, 2000, pp. 29-37.

Notes on Authors

Rosemary Betterton is Reader in Women's Studies at Lancaster University and writes widely on the areas of feminist art, history and theory. She is the author of *Looking on: Images of Femininity in the Visual Arts*, and *Media and Intimate Distance: Women, Artists and the Body.*

Dr. Helen C. Chapman is Senior Lecturer in Philosophy at Staffordshire University. Her research interests include 18th century German philosophy, aspects of feminist philosophy and more recently the dialogue between fine art practice and aesthetics. She is author of *Memory in Perspective* in the *Nexus* series.

Dr. Gérald Cipriani lectures in Aesthetics at the University of Central England in Birmingham. Forthcoming publications include papers in *Art in the Making - Aesthetics, Historicity and Practice*. Peter Lang, Germany; *Philosophical Enquiry: An International Philosophical Quarterly*, Vol XXI.3, Greece; and *Ideas y Valores*. Revista Colombiana de Filosofia, Colombia.

Dr. Gen Doy is Professor of the History and Theory of Visual Culture at De Montfort University, Leicester. Her books include *Seeing and Consciousness: Women, Class, Representation*; *Materializing Art History*; and *Black Visual Culture: Modernity and Postmodernity.*

Dr. Penny Florence is Director of Research at Falmouth College of Arts and a film and video maker whose most recent work (with Jason Whittaker) is a Mallarmé poem spatially transposed onto CD-ROM. She is the author of *Mallarmé, Manet and Redon: Visual and Aural Signs and the Generation of Meaning*, and coeditor with Dee Reynolds of *Feminist Subjects, Multi-Media, Cultural Methodologies.*

Dr. Marsha Meskimmon is Senior Lecturer in the School of Art and Design at Loughborough University. She has jointly curated and contributed to a travelling exhibition 'Materialisations' with two artists, and was series editor of *Nexus*. Her books include *The Art of Reflection: Women Artists' Self-Portraiture in the Twentieth Century*, and *We Weren't Modern Enough: Women Artists and the Limits of German Modernism*.

Judy Purdom is completing a PhD at Warwick University and working on Deleuze and Painting. She has published articles on Deleuze and Merleau Ponty, contributed to *Third Text* and is co-editing *Going Australian; Feminism and Philosophy*, a forthcoming special edition of *Hypatia*.

John Roberts is a writer, lecturer and freelance curator who curated the travelling exhibition 'Renegotiations: Class, Modernity and Photography'. He is the author of *Postmodernism, Politics and Art*, and *Selected Errors: Writings on Art and Politics 1981-1990*. He is the editor of *Art Has No History! The Making and Unmaking of Modern Art*.

Jacquie Swift is a freelance artist and writer who has worked in several universities and colleges. In addition to organising conferences at the University of West of England and the University of Central England she has been a guest editor of *Drawing Fire*, editor of *Art Education Discourses* and is co-editor with John Swift of *Disciplines, Fields and Change in Art Education*.

.